ESCAPE OF THE
AMETHYST

C. E. Lucas Phillips

ESCAPE OF THE
AMETHYST

Published by Sapere Books.
20 Windermere Drive, Leeds, England, LS17 7UZ,
United Kingdom

saperebooks.com

ISBN: 978-1-80055-281-4.

TABLE OF CONTENTS

AUTHOR'S NOTE

This account of the extraordinary exploit of HMS *Amethyst* in the River Yangtse in 1949 — described by the Commander-in-Chief as an 'epic in the history of the Navy' — has been compiled from official papers and from responsible personal narratives of some of those who took part in it.

In swift and confused actions, and particularly under the stresses to which all hands of the *Amethyst* were subjected, it is inevitable that there will be some conflict of evidence about who did what, and when, together with some complete gaps in evidence altogether. These doubts, however, are only in minor matters and wherever they have arisen I have tried to record events according to the balance of the best evidence available.

The titles and ranks that are used are those appropriate to the time.

I am grateful to the Admiralty for the facilities that they have so kindly placed at my disposal and for the ready help of the members of the staff at all times. I tender my cordial thanks also to all those who have personally informed and guided me, including Admiral Sir Patrick Brind, GBE, KGB, Admiral Sir Alexander Madden, KCB, GBE, Sir Ralph Stevenson, GCMG, Mr G. L. Weston, DSG, RN (retd.), Major R. V. Dewar-Durie, Mr E. L. Monaghan, RN, Acting Chief Petty Officer L. Frank, DSM (especially for permission to use his personal diary), Mr M. E. Fearnley, DSG, MD, Miss Charlotte Dunlap (now in Formosa), Mr D. G. Heath, RN and Dr Lin Yu-tang, the distinguished Chinese author, for so kindly reading Chapter 1 and advising me on Chinese spellings.

Above all, however, I am indebted to Commander J. S. Kerans, DSO, RN, without whose ready co-operation it would not have been possible to write so complete an account of an exploit in which he himself played so distinguished and remarkable a part.

C. E. L. P.

Faith is not the least of the lessons to be learnt when in adversity — COMMANDER J. S. KERANS, DSO, RN

Whatever the Captain decides, he can rest assured that we are all with him and shall not let him down — ACTING CHIEF PETTY OFFICER L. FRANK, DSM

This incident was certainly in the tradition of the Royal Navy — an honour and an inspiration to rising generations — MISS CHARLOTTE DUNLAP, *American medical missionary*

PART ONE: LAWFUL OCCASION

CHAPTER 1: SHEPHERD'S WARNING

OVER THE dun landscape of the valley of the Yangtse Kiang the sun rose red on the April mornings of 1949. The peasant on the southern bank, as he plodded out to his little field, the coolie as he took up his load, the merchant as he sorted his wares, looked upon it with fear or with misgiving or perhaps with some spark of hope. For the Red armies of Northern China, sweeping down from their bitter plains and flowing over the silken lands of Shantung, now stood upon the northern bank of the Yangtse, ready to cross.

What threat or what promise lay hidden behind that vast red staining of the sky? Would there be at long last a release from the chains of the usurer, the landlord and the corrupt official? Or would these ancient tyrannies continue in a new habit under the name of 'liberation'.

For thirty-eight years China had been torn by war. An ancient people, long schooled in the doctrine of 'wise passiveness', accustomed through the centuries to enduring foreign conquest with equanimity, lacking, for the greater part, any concept of nationhood, had been thrown into the maelstrom of strange new ideas. Their land had become a battleground upon which their souls, or the lure of their possessions, had been fought for again and again, not only by a few true patriots but also by rival gangs of brigand warlords and by the atrocious Japanese. What profit had come to the people since Dr Sun Yat-sen, drinking deep of western ideas, had overthrown the Manchu dynasty in 1911? The shabby republic that he had fathered had been at war since its infancy. There had been his own struggle with his Imperial rival, Yuan

Shih-kai. After their deaths what had begun as a patriotic conflict degenerated into a confused, ignoble turmoil in which rival and treacherous war-lords, still mouthing the catchwords of patriotism, fought one another with rabble armies, each defending against his competitors the territory that he had grasped for himself and each clamping upon the poor new bondages and barbarities more galling than the old.

Parallel with this black line in the graph of China's history there had developed other lines of brighter hue and higher motive. One was the great patriot movement, founded by Sun Yat-sen, known as the Kuomintang, the party of the National Revolution, the broad objects of which had been to rouse China to a sense of nationhood, to abolish ancient oppressions and foreign dominations and to establish a form of popular government.

Quite early there shone forth among Sun's followers the trim figure of the brilliant young officer Chiang Kai-shek, and upon his shoulders the mantle of the leader was draped upon the death of Sun. In a campaign of fanatical enthusiasm he led the improvised Nationalist armies from the far south of Canton to the gates of Shanghai and on to Pekin, vanquishing the war-lords, arousing national fervour and bringing China to the brink of war with the West. Only the steadiness and restraint of Major-General John Duncan's special brigade in Shanghai saved the peace. Patriotic, inflexible, stiff-necked, a Christian like Sun, Chiang was to be the spindle round which the whirligig of China's destiny was to revolve for a whole generation to come; and not least of the tensions and springs that was to influence the spinning of that roundabout was the abiding hate of Russia and of Communism that was born in him after a visit to Moscow. For, although the Kuomintang was modelled on the methods and machinery of the Russian

Communist Party (a fact that recurs to one today with some cynical surprise) and continued to derive much of its tactical guidance from the Moscow revolution, Chiang, a passionate Nationalist, was convinced that the Russians were scheming to tear China to pieces for their own ultimate profit.

This dark hatred and suspicion was the main obstacle that separated the Kuomintang from the other parallel movement in the affairs of China — the Chinese Communist Party. The Kuomintang copied the Russians only in organisation and method, not in doctrine. Both bodies sought the objective of the dominance and rule of a single party. But with the example of Russia brought so near, it was inevitable that the smoky lamp of Communism, though lit far away in London by a muddle-headed German in exile, should in the minds of a confused people seem to glow with a new hope and a new promise. They had seen it burst into a blinding incandescence in Czarist Russia, successfully burning to cinders an ancient way of life. To those in China who likewise wished to destroy an ancient way — both to the would-be war-lords and to the men of simpler faith who became disillusioned by the Kuomintang's failure to fulfil its early pledges of reform — the Bolsheviks seemed to point the way. Thus it was that in 1921 the Communist Party was founded in China. Its links with Russia were slender, and Moscow frowned upon its methods, for it was an agrarian movement, making its main appeal to the peasants, and in Russian doctrine peasants were bad material for Communism. The Chinese Communists, therefore, pursued their own way, and for many years it was a hard and stony one. Russia officially maintained a 'correct' attitude between the two elements, her Embassy always moving with the Government of China, that is to say, with Chiang Kai-shek.

At first only a political party within the national state and sharing in the common fight, the Communists were exorcised by Chiang after the march on Shanghai, escaping extermination only by flight into remote and rugged fastnesses, and it was in adversity that they built their strength. At length, after the fabulous 'Long March' and after much violence and outrage, they carved out for themselves a stronghold in the far north province of Shensi, and there they built up something like a war-lord's domain, sometimes acknowledging the suzerainty of the Kuomintang, at others defying it, as suited them best.

As Chiang Kai-shek sprang to the leadership of the Nationalist Party, so in the Communist Party the figure that came early to the fore was Mao Tse-tung, slab-faced, ruthless, cold-blooded, physically and mentally tough, hated of Chiang from an early date. Mao was of modest origins, but his two most significant associates — the future foreign minister, Chou En-lai, and the professional soldier, General Chu Teh — were by no means so.

These rivalries of war-lords, and of Kuomintang and Communists, held China in division for many years until there came a menace from without that suddenly gave promise of unity in the face of a common adversity. In 1937 the Japanese, in contempt of the League of Nations and in flagrant pursuit of gainful aggression already cynically accomplished in Manchuria, invaded China proper. Miraculously, war-lords, Kuomintang and Communists all came together, somewhat hesitantly, in a common cause under the leadership of Chiang. It was an uneasy alliance and unsuccessful in its purpose of expelling the Japanese (as the Communists knew it must be), but it saved the soul of China. Superior in every point, the Japanese poured south from Manchuria, over-running great stretches of China. The Communist Army, conducting a guerrilla war in the north, remained physically separated from the government forces, who were pressed back southwards in a stale and sterile defensive for seven years. Pearl Harbour came and China found powerful new friends, especially the generous friendship of the United States, together with the less opulent help of Great Britain. But nothing availed to stem the bloodthirsty conquests of the Japanese, nor could all the spurrings of General Stilwell prick the Nationalists from their soul-destroying static position. They waited passively for the Americans to beat the common enemy for them, and at last in the fateful summer of 1945 the first atomic bombs in history accomplished this desirable purpose for them. The Japanese laid down their arms and the Chinese Government returned from its hiding place in far Chungking, back to its old capital of Nanking. To Nanking accordingly likewise went the foreign embassies, our own, of course, with them — and the Russian also. There also, in pursuance of our treaty rights freely negotiated and respected by all the contending forces of China, went the destroyers, sloops or frigates of the Royal Navy, to act as guard-ships for the maintenance of the Embassy and for the protection of all British Commonwealth communities.

To Chiang and Mao the alliance against Japan was merely an interruption, a putting into cold storage, of their own internal struggle, and as soon as Japan had been brought to her knees by America the old bickerings began again. But in how different a temper and with how much more meaning and purpose! For the Japanese war had administered to the Communists and to the Nationalists two quite different medicines — to the one a stimulus, to the other a sedative. The Communists, in their lone guerrilla war in the north, virtually unaided and dependent on their own resourcefulness, emerged under General Chu Teh, a hardened, disciplined, cold-blooded, determined force. They armed themselves with equipment captured from the Japanese, and later with American equipment captured from the Nationalists. They had no aircraft. The Nationalists, by contrast, despite the equipment provided for them by America, despite the support and advice of American generals and diplomats, emerged with their revolutionary fervour dimmed by the sterile years, their faith shaken by promises long unfulfilled, their discipline and loyalty slackened by divided and querulous leadership. Corruption ate deep into their being. Chiang Kai-shek, Generalissimo and now President of the Republic, though himself always honest, had, after years of autocracy, become obdurate and narrow-visioned, seeing the world through the blinkers of his own hates and conceits.

By 1947 the new Communist armies were already on the march in the north in open revolt against the government. They struck hard and often and everywhere the Nationalists crumpled before them. Manchuria fell to them. Peking fell, Tientsin fell. Rich with the booty of captured arms, their forces, under the propagandist title of 'China People's Liberation Army', pressed relentlessly to the south, fought a great, fluctuating battle of encirclement at Suchow, and drove the Nationalists in flight far south to the great natural obstacle of the Yangtse River. There, in the spring of 1949, the two armies sat and glared at each other across the waters along a front of several hundred miles, while the government made desperate efforts to persuade the Communists to come to terms. The Nationalists, vacillating and divided, were by now a nearly spent force. Their leaders had proved incapable of meeting the crisis that faced them. Chiang retired from the Presidency, whose hard duties now fell upon the Vice-President, General Li Tsung-jen, a liberal and one of the few victors in battle against the Japanese. The cabinet decamped from Nanking back to Canton, but Li, ready to sacrifice his own body for the cause in answer to the Communists' call for revengeful blood, remained at the capital, separated from his enemies by nothing but the waters of the Yangtse. So, too, did the British, American and many other embassies.

The Yangtse Kiang, or 'Long River', is one of the great waterways of the world. What the Nile is to Egypt, the St. Lawrence to Canada, the Mississippi to the United States, so is the Yangtse to China. Rising far away in the secret mountains of Tibet, its source embosomed in sumptuous, tumbling woods of rhododendron, primula and Himalayan poppy, it traverses the whole of central China in its great sweep of 3400 miles, giving life and being to 200 million souls in the unnumbered towns and villages clustered along its course, till at last, in a twenty-mile wide estuary, it pours its grey-brown waters into the East China Sea immediately north of Shanghai.

For the greater part of its course the Yangtse runs through great mountain areas, racing between steep rocky sides or tumbling through narrow gorges, but every now and then swirling widely through rich, alluvial basins and verdant valleys. As it nears the sea at Chinkiang, the point at which it makes its entrance into our story, it broadens out into a mile-wide flood, following a serpentine course through flat, marshy country, its waters stained the colour of milk chocolate by its heavy load of alluvial silt and impeded by innumerable islands and sandbanks that vex the way of the navigator. This is the Yangtse — the Yangtse of the low-lying province of Kiangsu, from the ancient walled city of Chinkiang to the open sea — upon whose waters and along whose banks we shall live and move in this story.

Those who sailed with Skinner in the *Amethyst* on his last voyage, on those broad, grey-brown waters, fast-flowing and tidal, looked out upon a busy and diversified scene. Flocks of ducks drifted by, making their unpaid-for passage economically to market or the canning factory. Once in a while the sad corpse of an unwanted female baby, like a broken water-lily, floated at the whim of the changeful tides. Great rafts of logs, nursed by little tugs, came down-river from the inland forests. Shipping of many kinds made passage to and fro. Small sampans, punt-like, their sterns often covered with domes of matting, loaded with merchandise or family goods, were propelled slowly in the shallows by a single oar in the stern by the method of propulsion known in China as *yu-lohing*. Their teams of cormorants, with which the boatmen caught their bony fish, were grouped idly upon the gunwale, or darted suddenly into the depths like some relentless water hawk. Junks of all sizes sailed back and forth under their great, square sails of matting or canvas, their blunt bows and high freeboard belying to European eyes their qualities of seaworthiness. Steamers of all sorts plied a busy traffic of passengers or goods. And every now and then, sleeker, faster, cleaner than any of these, there went upon her lawful treaty occasions a warship of some friendly foreign power.

The passenger upon this busy waterway to be traversed by the *Amethyst* sees along its shores an equally diversified scene. Along both banks old forts, if they are visible, give evidence of warlike measures. To the north, especially along the Kou An Reach, which will shortly come violently into our vision, all is flat, sometimes marshy, but intensively cultivated and dappled with the Cunningham firs, the bamboo groves, the cinnamon, the camphor and the cryptomeria that surround the little homesteads, or with the maidenhair tree, the horsetail pine and the sweet gum that embower the shrines of ancestors. Here and there groves of white mulberry trees, upon which the silkworm feeds, testify to one of the most ancient of Chinese industries, taught to her people by the goddess-wife of the great Yellow Emperor of ancient myth. From behind such quiet groves and peaceful coppices we shall soon see the flashes of the guns that assailed the *Amethyst*.

Look southward now. Here, from old Chinkiang eastward, standing a little back from the low banks of the river, two fingers of rocky hills stretch out, last evidence of the great mountains through which the Yangtse has run its course, ancient outposts of land in the sea that once covered these parts. They rise sharply from the flat, dyke-crossed country and make of the south shore a rougher landscape than the one which faces it, as Kerans and the American doctor were to discover when they went by night to succour the wounded. No roads traverse it other than rude tracks. At the extremity of Tuan Shan stands an old pagoda, with old guardian forts at the foot, and dotted along the range are little temples and shrines of ancestors and little farmsteads, each enfolded in its grove of trees or shrubs. Here the pheasant and the pigeon fly and here the silver crescents of the rice fields gleam under the summer moon.

In this fertile land of Kiangsu, on the latitude of Cairo, of New Orleans and of the Canaries, north and south meet in a profitable marriage. The chestnut and the maple mingle with the palm, the bamboo and with fragrant camphor woods. In the winter the farmer grows wheat and beans, and in the sultry, humid summer, rice, tea and cotton. All the earth that is not too swampy is intensively cultivated, and the urban areas are surrounded by belts of vegetable gardens to their very walls in a network of ditches and canals, their waters fed upon by multitudes of duck, their banks noisy with the croaking of the frog and the night air swarming with mosquitoes.

All this busy land is thronged by a smiling, humorous and likeable people, rippling with laughter as someone parodies a pompous official or a 'big nose' foreigner. They are garmented, for the greater part, in sombre blue or black, giving, it would seem, greater point to their native wit. The coolie on the riverside, under his huge straw hat, carrying twin burdens from a wooden yoke fore-and-aft across one shoulder, trudges to and fro, chanting his eternal singsong of the ages. The chattering women, crow-black hair varnished and coiled, stoop over the crops in the fields or with full, brown breasts suckle their babies at the village doors. At the roadside pigs squeal and wallow in the dust and the small hens scrabble and complain. A laden wheelbarrow, with twin troughs flanking its great four-foot wheel, trundles into sight, the good man pushing it and his wife pulling in front on a rope. An old woman rides by, pickaback on the shoulders of her strong son. Everywhere there is that characteristic muffled sound of China — the padding and the shuffling of feet in the dust. In the evening — as the men of the *Amethyst* were to see for a hundred nights — when the frogs begin to croak and the men come home from work in the dusk, a haze of blue smoke rises from the villages as the evening meal is cooked and the aroma of Chinese cooking gives refreshing challenge to the smell of human bodies and to the obscene emanations from the excreta pits of a people who return to the land all that they have taken from it.

But now, in the spring of 1949, all this pleasant land is anxious and distracted. For months it has been filled with soldiers. It has been filled also with numberless refugees from the Communists, crowding in insanitary squalor in every city and village. Along a front of several hundred miles the Communist armies, clad in their mustard uniforms, stand on the north side, their guns covering the banks, their fleets of junks, which they will use for the assault crossing in lieu of the modern landing craft that they do not possess, concealed in the innumerable creeks. On the south bank the Nationalist forces, in drab olive-green, face them, outwardly calm but their cohesion and their confidence shaken. No guns fire, for there is a truce while the distracted Nationalist leaders consider the ultimatum that has been presented to them — an ultimatum such as none could accept, for, in the Communist manner, it demands blood. The Acting President, Li Tsung-jen, has offered his own blood, has offered to take all responsibility and to be himself declared a 'war criminal', but that will not do. Mao lusts for the head of Chiang Kai-shek.

Some shipping continues to move on the Yangtse, including small warships of the Nationalist navy, but an air of doom broods over all the landscape as the *Amethyst* begins to approach from the east.

CHAPTER 2: MEET THE *AMETHYST*

HIS MAJESTY'S ship *Amethyst*, of the Third Frigate Flotilla, at the time of her strange adventure was a very junior unit in the Far East Fleet. That Fleet, though charged with a very large responsibility, ranging from Indonesia to Japan, was a relatively small one, its largest ships being the cruisers *London* and *Belfast*, each of 10,000 tons, and the calls upon all ships were heavy. As Commander-in-Chief Far East Station their lordships of the Admiralty had appointed Admiral Sir Patrick Brind, KCB, CBE, one of the Royal Navy's most popular Flag officers. He was to be found usually far away at Singapore, sometimes at Hong Kong and sometimes at sea, but we shall see his distant, tall figure doing all it can do to influence and direct the course of the extraordinary events, for which there was no textbook and no precedent.

Second to Admiral Brind, with the designation of Flag Officer Second-in-Command Far East Station, which we shall compress navywise to FO2, was Vice-Admiral A. C. G. Madden, CB, CBE, who at the period of our story was conveniently moving up from Hong Kong to Shanghai for the St George's Day celebrations and whom we shall see constantly in the background and, indeed, making a gallant effort to get from there into the front.

One of the responsibilities of the Far East Fleet was to provide the recognised guard-ship at Nanking, the seat of the Chinese Government, some two hundred miles up the Yangtse from Shanghai. Here was to be found our Embassy, with Sir Ralph Stevenson, GCMG, square, dark and brisk of manner, in the office of Ambassador, and Mr Lionel Lamb as Minister.

His Naval Attaché, and Senior Service Attaché, was Captain V. D'A. Donaldson, and as Assistant Naval Attaché we meet the slender, shrewd, significant figure of Lieutenant-Commander John Kerans, whom we shall see thrust suddenly from the roses and armchairs of the Embassy into one of the roughest situations in which a naval officer has found himself, but in which he was to show himself, by one of those happy circumstances that the Royal Navy has not seldom provided, as the right man in the right place at the right time.

In addition to our Embassy, there were also the diplomatic representatives of the Commonwealth and an appreciable British community of business and other interests. All these people, as we well knew from the experience of 1927, when Nanking had been sacked, were likely to be in considerable jeopardy and scarcity if the situation should get out of hand during the contact stage of the civil law. It was for this reason that we maintained a guard-ship at the capital. We did so by virtue of old treaty rights, honoured by successive Chinese governments and honoured even by the Japanese during their occupation before Pearl Harbour; and, indeed, Mr Attlee, the Prime Minister, had, some time before, specially asked that the provision of this guard-ship should be maintained.

The first serious threat to Nanking had been in early November and this had prompted Stevenson to ask the Commander-in-Chief of that time, Admiral Sir Denis Boyd, KGB, GBE, DSG, if he could furnish a guard-ship to bring essential supplies, to provide a stabilising influence if conditions deteriorated, and be prepared to evacuate the British communities. To this Boyd had agreed and the first ship that had been sent had, in fact, been *Amethyst* herself. Her presence, and that of all her successors, had been warmly appreciated and had had a steadying influence on all communities. The sanction of the Chinese Nationalist Government was, of course, obtained; and Boyd had been anxious to confirm the assent of the insurgent armies also, but the Communists themselves had made it impossible to contact them.

To all these people moving in the currents of higher policy, HMS *Amethyst*, before she leapt from her obscurity into the headlines of the world's press, was but small fry. She was no powerful vessel of offence. Her normal duties were rather those of watch and ward in protective capacities, especially protection against submarines, and her weapons, whether anti-submarine, anti-aircraft or main armament for surface targets, were such as would serve for the defence of a convoy or the protection of the King's subjects overseas. Eighth of her name and launched in 1943, she was of the 'later *Black Swan*' class, originally rated as sloops but afterwards designated frigates. She had sunk a German submarine off the coast of Ireland in 1945, had been present at the Japanese surrender in New Guinea, and after the war had taken part in the mission of mercy to Japanese earthquake victims. She displaced 1495 tons and measured a few inches short of 300 feet overall, with a beam of 38 feet, and had been built by Alexander Stephen & Sons on the Clyde. Her main armament was six 4-inch dual-purpose[1] guns mounted in pairs behind the partial protection of armoured shields which did not totally enclose the guns and did not therefore claim the title of turrets. Two pairs of these twin guns, known as A gun and B gun, were mounted forward of the ship's bridge, and the third pair, known as X gun, was mounted aft, firing over the quarterdeck and, of course, to port and starboard as well as overhead. Against aircraft specifically the frigate carried two twin 40-millimetre Bofors guns and two

---

[1] Designed and mounted to engage both surface and aerial targets.

single Oerlikons, small quick-firing heavy machine guns. Except on her gun shields, she had no armour-plating. Her oil-fuelled turbines gave her, in practice, a maximum speed of eighteen knots. Her peacetime complement was 170 officers and ratings and these included, as is usual in HM ships in these waters, a certain number of Chinese ratings employed as stewards and cooks, together with civilian tradesmen such as tailors and laundrymen, allowed on board for such trade as they could make.

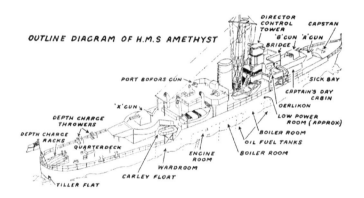

To most landsmen nearly every ship of war appears impossibly cramped and crowded with gear. You bump your head and stub your toe and lose your way. You wonder by what secret sense the seaman moves with such sure ease and freedom. It is a world of bare, hard steel in which the sailor alone knows how to discover comfort. Imagine *Amethyst* very much in this sort. In her small hull are crowded not only all the trappings of an ocean-going ship, but also much of the fighting gear of a larger ship of war. Below decks, even in a plan, the landsman's eye is confused by the honeycomb of cabins, messes, lockers, stores of all sorts, power plant, engine-room and fuel tanks, sick bay, fire-fighting gear, ammunition hoists, fan vents and motors and the serried ranks of vital cables, pipes and tubes that wander along every bulkhead. An enormous amount of the ship's life, both domestic and operational, is conducted by electricity — the lighting, heating, ventilation, cooling (so vital in tropical waters), food storage, the wireless, the radar, the firing of the guns, the searchlights, the pumping, the extremely important internal communication systems and much else besides, the viability of which is to prove of critical importance to *Amethyst* in her plight.

We have no time to go over all these organs and mechanisms of the ship's life, but in order to follow the swift and crowded events of our narrative we must quickly inspect that important superstructure built forward of the single mast where we shall find the heart and nerve-centre of the whole ship. Surmounting this superstructure is the director-tower in which the long-armed Barr and Stroud range-finder is located and from which the Gunnery Control Officer directs the fire of the guns. Below this is the bridge, command post of the whole ship. It is entirely open and exposed and its extreme vulnerability is to have the most critical results the very moment the guns begin to fire. Here are the magnetic compass and the pelorus, which shows the reading of the gyro-compass below-deck. From the bridge the captain has communication with several parts of the ship, but particularly with the engine-room, director and wheelhouse, by means of direct voice-pipes or telephones.

Immediately below the bridge is the wheelhouse, and of this also we shall see the critical, and indeed tragic, import. Here, receiving orders from the bridge by voice-pipe, the coxswain stands at the wheel, flanked on either hand by seamen who man the port and starboard engine-room telegraphs and the engine revolution-counter. Unlike the bridge, the wheelhouse is almost totally enclosed and the coxswain does not see what lies ahead but steers according to orders that he receives from the bridge by voice-pipe. In like manner, the hands manning the telegraphs set their pointers in accordance with voice-pipe orders from the bridge and these settings are mechanically conveyed to the engine-room below for the manipulation of the port and starboard propellers respectively; for the twin propellers can be employed not only to drive the ship direct ahead or astern, but also to execute a turning movement, with or without the wheel. If the normal 'forward' steering from the wheelhouse should break down, the ship can also be steered, but with much greater difficulty, from the tiller-flat, a half-deck or platform in the extreme stern of the ship on the lower deck. We shall see this being done when *Consort* tries to come to the aid of *Amethyst*.

Abaft, or behind, the wheelhouse is the captain's small sea-cabin. Abaft of that again is the charthouse, where, besides its obvious appurtenances, is also to be found the echo-sounder, which, by recording the readings of electric impulses, tells the captain the depth of water beneath the ship. The readings are called out to the bridge above by voice-pipe. This echo-sounder, in the shoal-infested waters of the Yangtse, with no pilot and with Chinese charts, was to prove one of the ship's most trusty friends in the great race of her life.

Below the charthouse are two other important organs of the ship's being. On the port side is the wireless office, which speaks for itself but which was to be much more than its name implies, and in which we shall see Telegraphist French, sole man of his trade on board, performing prodigies of endurance. From here the ship can communicate over the air either by wireless telegraphy in the Morse code or, for short distances, by voice on the radio-telephone. On the starboard side below the charthouse is the transmitting station. This is the instrumental link between the director and the guns, and here are applied the corrections, due to temperature and other factors, for the range and direction of the target as read on the range-finder in the director-control tower above.

In this superstructure, then, we have seen those organs of the ship from which tactical and navigational command is effected. Equally vital to the ship, and to our narrative, are her engines and machinery. We need not yet actually go down into her engine- and boiler-rooms, nor enter upon technicalities, but in order to follow the fortunes of the ship with understanding and to see how in the end they determined her destiny, we must have some idea of the sources of power that enabled her to live and move and keep touch with the outside world from which she was to be physically cut off for so long.

Her engines were used not only to propel the ship, but also to maintain the daily life of all on board. These all-steel honeycombs, even long before the thermometers ashore reach the 100 degrees mark, and with a humidity of 80 per cent saturation as it is in high summer in the province of Kiangsu, become floating furnaces, in which human activity becomes nearly impossible, unless means are provided for preserving food, manufacturing fresh water and providing some degree of bodily coolness. Prickly heat tortures the skin, men faint at their work below decks and may die of heatstroke. Only strict obedience to the disciplines of health and hygiene enables them to support it for prolonged periods. Once disease comes in, or hygiene deteriorates or vermin appear, then there is immediate peril. More obviously there is peril if the ship cannot steam, or fire her guns, or provide fresh water and pure food, or communicate with the world. For these reasons the supply of fuel and the activity of her engines are needed even when the ship rides idle.

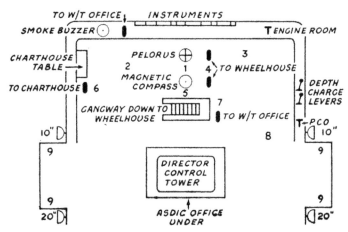

■ *VOICE-PIPE*   **T** *TELEPHONE*   D *SEARCHLIGHT PROJECTOR*

Diagram of layout of *Amethyst*'s bridge. The numerals represent typical action stations — 1. Captain; 2. Navigating Officers; 3. Action Officer of the Watch; 4. Pilot; 5. Number One; 6. Navigator, Yeoman; 7. Signalman; 8. Yeoman of Signals; 9. Lookouts.

Amethyst's motive power was derived from turbines driven by steam supplied by oil-fired boilers. The vital electric services were provided from turbo-generators powered by the same means. When the ship was in harbour and it was wasteful to keep her boilers alight, electricity was supplied by an independent diesel generator, but in the great trial of which we are to be spectators her diesel generator was out of action, so that, whenever electricity was needed, the boilers had to be 'flashed up' to raise steam to drive the turbogenerators. This was to be a crucial factor in her predicament, and we shall see how exceedingly important was the maintenance of this electricity and how disaster could attend its breakdown. Both high power and low power circuits were provided. The high power, of 220 volts, drove the main machinery, fire and bilge pumps, ventilating fans, refrigerators, the ship's lighting, ammunition hoists and other services.

For the main wireless both high and low power circuits were necessary. Low power current was also used for the ship's internal communication systems, for the navigational and gunnery control instruments, for auxiliary lighting and for the very important gyro-compass, that fast-spinning wheel low in the ship, with its 'repeaters' on bridge and in wheelhouse, which helped to maintain accurate navigation.

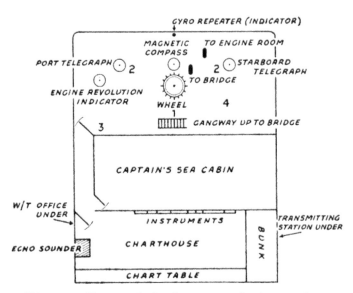

Diagram of layout of wheelhouse, etc. Stations — 1. Coxswain; 2. Telegraphsmen; 3. Boatswain's mate; 4. Quartermaster.

The nerve-centre for all these latter services was the low-power room, which comes prominently into our story, and you may imagine it as a sort of robot-looking room containing nothing but a few instruments and a board with rows of switches and dials. In addition to these means of providing power, the ship also carried, in the event of breakdown, electric batteries for all vital equipment, including wireless equipment.

Not everything, however, was done by electricity. Some of the essential services were provided by small oil-driven engines or pumps. The most vital of these was the evaporator, which distilled fresh water from the sea or river; if that had broken down during *Amethyst*'s captivity there would have been immediate disaster. Pumps also provided pressure for flushing the 'heads' or lavatories and for the circulation of water to showerbaths and washbasins. The cooking stoves in the galleys were also oil-fired but were quite separate from the ship's engines.

Thus, as long as food, fresh water and fuel last, this well-found ship, as crowded and busy as a steel beehive, is a little world to itself, equipped in all the needs of life; yet, while her communications hold, intimately in touch with all the world and able to converse across the oceans. Unlike the ships of old, therefore, however remote she may be, she is as completely subject to the orders of her superiors as though they lay alongside each other, and her captain does not have that entire independence of action and that free initiative to use his own judgment that have so often in olden times made the captain of a ship the decisive dictator of events. Only on quite extraordinary occasions, as in *Amethyst*'s adventure, is her captain able to exercise a large degree of freedom and responsibility.

All these things indicate the heavy responsibility of a ship's captain when isolated from the world and the multitude of matters to which he must give his mind at one and the same time. But, above all technicalities, supported by the First Lieutenant, he must keep his finger on the pulse of the men under his command, alert not only to the health of their bodies but also to the state of their minds and the strength of their hearts. He must know just what is the apparent limit of his men's endurance, and be able to lead them, if necessary, a little beyond it. All this we shall see put to the proof in the *Amethyst*.

Imagine the *Amethyst*, then, as a small, fairly modern ship, somewhat cramped, designed chiefly for light protective duties and for only limited offensive action, well fitted to sustain human life in a hot and humid climate as long as her electrical gear does not fail. We see her first at the end of February 1949, under the command of Lieutenant-Commander B. M. Skinner, steaming away from Malaya, where she had been on anti-bandit patrol off the east coast in co-operation with our land and air forces, making for Hong Kong, some 1440 miles away to the north-east, for annual refit. On arrival at Hong Kong, however, her programme was changed. By one of those trivial quirks of circumstance 30 that so often alter the destinies of men and nations, it was decided to substitute her for HM Australian Ship *Shoalhaven* in the relief of the destroyer *Consort* (Commander I. G. Robertson, DSO, DSC) as guard-ship at Nanking. *Consort*'s relief was long overdue and had been put off more than once on account of the international situation, but the state of her provisioning was causing some concern and the change must be made as soon as possible now that there was a truce between the rival armies.

Amethyst's departure from Hong Kong was delayed for a while, however, in order to take on board two new officers and thirty ratings due out from home in the troopship *Dunera* in exchange for others due for relief, including some 'great characters' whom she was sorry to lose. Thus she acquired a new Navigating Officer in Lieutenant (ND) P. E. C. Berger and a new Engineer Officer in Lieutenant (E) E. G. Wilkinson. Having embarked these, together with a quantity of Imperial War Graves tombstones for Shanghai that inspired appropriate lower deck observations, and leaving a Bofors gun behind in Hong Kong for repair, she sailed for Shanghai on April 12th, a passage of 860 miles, and, arriving there on the 15th, saw again the great, grey-brown flood of the Yangtse pouring its waters many miles out into the blue expanse of the sea. For to most of the ship's company the Yangtse was a familiar scene, and in their previous tour of duty as guard-ship at Nanking they had in fact re-built the new wharf, hard by the big egg factory of the International Export Company at the suburb of Hogee, where *Consort* at that moment lay. There was no great enthusiasm at the return there, for the great, oft-ravaged city, with the notorious excreta boats passing along its waterways, had, for the greater part, long forgotten whatever ancient lure and grandeur she may have possessed and was now but a raddled old woman who had little of charm or distraction to offer the visiting British sailor beyond contemplation of the lotus lakes and the tomb of Sun Yat-sen.

Shanghai, however, was different. Here they found that spring was well advanced but that the humidity of the Yangtse estuary had not yet reached the pitch where it saps the energy and the will. It was the most pleasant season of the year. In some distant gardens the flowering trees and shrubs that enrich the Chinese scene were in their splendour. On the wharves and in the streets they heard again the chattering of innumerable tongues, for in this great, throbbing, cosmopolitan city, built by European genius out of the marshes, the nations of the world meet at the crossroads of commerce. The uniforms of the great navies and of the shipping lines of the world mingled with those of the sailors and soldiers of the Chinese Nationalist forces, with the lounge suits and frocks of European civilians and with the varied garments of the Chinese of all classes. The rickshaw mixed with tram and car and lorry, and the gay, painted signs of the Chinese shops vied with the great European stores.

This kaleidoscope, this hum and throb of the great city, presented itself to the young men of the little frigate. Over the sights and sounds and smells there hung an air of suspended crisis, as the great contest between the government forces and the approaching Communists was anxiously watched. The crisis had hung in the sky for some months now and had become a little stale, but all knew that the time must be near when it would be resolved and that there was not likely to be a further postponement of the D-day of the Communists.

It was to conform with these truce dates that the relief of *Consort* was carefully considered in such a way as not to become involved in the hostilities. In their passages up and down the river both ships would, of course, be passing between the two rival armies, and the British Ambassador in Nanking was anxious that the relief should take place while the truce still held, or, if that were impossible, delayed until after the Communists had successfully crossed the Yangtse, as everyone expected them to do. At the peace talks in Peking the Communists had made new and devastating demands on the government, including 'unconditional surrender', and had announced that, if these demands were not satisfied, they would attack across the Yangtse on April 12th. Nanking would be occupied on April 16th. Sir Ralph Stevenson had at that time accordingly asked Admiral Madden (in the absence of Admiral Brind, the Commander-in-Chief, in England for exercise 'Trident') that *Consort* should not then be relieved. Madden concurred, but asked for reconsideration on the 16th.

The Communists did not carry out their threat on the 12th, as General Li Tsung-jen made fresh efforts to save the day, but on the 17th they announced that April 20th would be the last day for the acceptance of their 'peace programme', or they would cross the Yangtse on the 21st. The consent of the Chinese Government having been obtained, it was accordingly arranged between Stevenson and Madden that the relief should take place within this new period of grace. It was appreciated (how rightly!) that, whatever guard-ship might be at Nanking, once the Communists were there it was likely to take a long time to get their permission to leave; and it was therefore specially important to get *Consort* out and replaced by a guard-ship provisioned for a long stay.

Unfortunately, it was quite impossible to discover the Communists' views. They themselves had made it so. Ever since their rebellion had begun they had shown a cold and persistent refusal — a 'stone wall of indifference' as Donaldson put it — to have anything whatever to do with any of our diplomatic representatives. Communications on any subject by our Consul left in Peking and Consul-General in Tientsin were bleakly ignored. The unfortunate diplomats, remaining at their stations, were cut off from the world by all means except wireless, marooned in an arctic sea of inattention. Had the Communists wished to put forward any views, all they had to do, as the Prime Minister pointed out later, was to convey them to our Consul at Peking.

There was, however, a perfectly clear assumption of assent from the fact that there had been no trouble about previous reliefs. HM ships had passed up and down the river between the two armies molested by no more than an occasional random shot fired by some irresponsible element of one side or the other. Admiral Brind had himself passed to Nanking and back in the *Alert*, his dispatch vessel, only some three weeks before, when Stevenson had laid emphasis on the value of the guard-ship to all the communities there. American warships had occasionally gone up, and a ship of the Indian Navy. All this had been quite in keeping with the behaviour of rival Chinese armies for a generation, for whenever the representatives of a neutral foreign power had wanted to pass through disputed areas the Chinese, like policemen holding up traffic, had always been prepared to stop the war for them. So long as one went about one's business in a quiet way, they did not interfere.

Thus the Communists, no less than the government, had always, so far as the Yangtse was concerned, given the appearance of respecting our treaty rights, and had not questioned the passage of our guard-ship. Britain, on her part, though her Embassy was necessarily at the seat of the Chinese Government, stood aside in strict neutrality in the quarrel, in accordance with the Moscow Declaration of 1945. So, too, did Russia and the United States, participants of the same declaration, their Embassies likewise at Nanking lending no aid to either side. It was China's affair. Our only concern was to maintain our Embassy and to provide for the safety of our own flesh and blood and the nationals of member states of the Commonwealth. If that should be imperilled, at Nanking or elsewhere within reach, it would be the business of the *Amethyst* to rescue them.

In the *Amethyst*, at Holt's Wharf, therefore, Skinner had no serious apprehensions. He was fully briefed by Commander John Pringle, the Assistant Naval Attaché, Shanghai, on the background of the situation as known there and as reported from Nanking. He knew, of course, that in his passage up the Yangtse he would have the Communists on his starboard hand and the Nationalists to port. The big river was a no-man's land, though the ships of the Chinese Navy held a large measure of control over it, for the Communists had no ships with which to challenge them. It was always possible that, in spite of our treaty rights and our neutrality, and in spite of the truce, some ignorant or 'trigger-happy' creature might let off a gun; and therefore, though not anticipating trouble, Skinner took the precautions that had been ordered by the Commander-in-Chief for all ships in these waters, both to emphasise his neutrality and to defend himself if need be. Large canvasses were painted with the Union Jack ready to be displayed over the ship's side. Ammunition was got up from the magazines with a view to closing up to action stations before reaching the danger area.

On April 18th Skinner received orders from the Senior British Naval Officer, afloat in Shanghai,[2] that *Amethyst* was to sail the next day. This would enable her to reach Nanking, and *Consort*, steaming at speed, to reach Kiang Yin, outside the trouble area, on the 20th; thus the relief would be completed before the Communists gave effect to their threat of renewing hostilities.

Before we leave Shanghai, however, let us meet some of the ship's company with whom we shall spend so much time.

---

[2] Captain A. D. H. Jay, DSO, DSG, Commanding 3rd Frigate Flotilla, in *Black Swan*.

As we have seen, the frigate was commanded by Lieutenant-Commander B. M. Skinner. Aged about thirty-five, he was short in stature, well-built, fair-haired and with a very ready smile. He had been born in Australia, the son of a Malaya rubber-planter, and before joining the Royal Navy in 1937 had served in the Blue Funnel line. He was one of the Navy's serious men, keen on his profession, and, had he lived, would certainly have gone far in it. To our loss, his part on our stage is all too short and he had already, while in Hong Kong, seen his wife for the last time.

The First Lieutenant, or 'Number One', was Lieutenant G. L. Weston, who had already won the Distinguished Service Cross in a landing operation against the Germans in the Mediterranean in 1944; to this DSG we shall soon see him adding a bar. Geoffrey Weston was the son of a brigadier-general of the First World War and was a naval officer of traditional stamp and style, trained at Dartmouth. Aged twenty-seven, he was fair-haired, stocky, square-rigged and looked a good rugger forward. He was a plain 'salt horse', who had followed no line of specialisation. He could be strict and downright but had that breeziness and cheerfulness of humour that one likes to associate with men of the sea, together with their custom of sticking to their guns at all costs.

The new 'Pilot', Lieutenant P. E. C. Berger, we have already seen coming on board at Hong Kong. Picture him as a tall, thin, slightly stooping figure, dark-haired, in character quiet and unassuming but with that inner spark and determination which in a dark hour was to win him the Distinguished Service Cross. Next in seniority was Lieutenant H. R. M. Mirehouse. Schooled at Harrow, he was an excellent messmate, amusing and lighthearted, unruffled in emergency. It was his business to run the ship's office. Like Skinner, both of these also, unhappily, will pass early out of our story.

Junior of the executive, or non-specialist, officers, who alone are qualified for duty on the bridge and command of the ship, was Lieutenant Stewart Hett. About twenty-two or twenty-three, he was small in stature, fresh-complexioned, fair-haired and still boyish in appearance. Rather shy, he had a quiet demeanour, a simple faith and a deep sense of loyalty. He never shouted, but leading by example quietly pressed on with his job. He was to be the only executive officer left alive and unwounded.

The new Engineer Officer, or 'Chief' to his messmates, we have also seen arriving at Hong Kong. 'Wilky' was a very experienced, ex-lower deck officer, slow-speaking, thoroughly genuine, undemonstrative and level-headed. Everyone liked him; and the ship's engines, with which we shall be much concerned, could not have been in better hands.

A recent arrival, not very long promoted from the lower deck, was Mr (Gunner) E. Monaghan, the Gunner, of that class now called Special Duties officers. An Irishman, as one would expect, 'the Gunner' was a likeable character and a thoroughly sound man at his job, which was the technical supervision of the ship's armament and the training of the gun crews; or, in action, to be in charge of the transmitting station. In the strange happenings to come, however, he showed a sailor-like promptness to turn his hand to any other job that had to be done.

The ship's doctor was Surgeon-Lieutenant J. M. Alderton, MB. A man of medium height, he wore a full ginger beard, was slow-speaking, and suggested the 'thoughtful Scot', though he was not one, with a quiet sense of humour. Coming from a medical family, he was first and foremost a professional doctor, but was also a man of remarkably cool and cheerful courage.

These were all the officers who were then with the ship, but a piece of extraordinarily good fortune at the last moment brought on board the Flotilla Electrical Officer, Lieutenant (L) G. B. Strain, as a passenger. On the eve of sailing from Shanghai, Skinner received a signal that he was to take passage in *Amethyst* to Nanking to overhaul the ship's radar and return in *Consort*. George Strain was very definitely a Scot, with a very agreeable Scots accent. He was a little fellow, bright-eyed and lively even in the darkest hour. He was not only a good technician but also an exceptionally fine officer. In the ship, but not of it, he was to be confronted with a critical situation that demanded something far more than technical qualifications, and he responded with courage, resource and initiative. He, Hett and Monaghan were to be the only officers not killed or wounded. 'He was,' said the First Lieutenant, at whose side he stood, 'a hell of a fine chap.'

Of the ratings in HMS *Amethyst* we have time to meet only a few before we go into action with them. Too many of the senior ratings, also, like the officers, will be dismissed the moment the curtain goes up. Thus we have only a brief glimpse of the coxswain and senior rating in the ship, the lean Chief Petty Officer Rosslyn Nicholls. The Chief Bo'sun's Mate (or 'Chief Buffer') and lord of the upper deck in seamanship matters, Chief Petty Officer David Heath, an exceptional young petty officer, was dragged off the stage by an unfortunate chance. Chief Engine-Room Artificer Stanley Roblin, a highly specialised rating, second only to the Engineer Officer, also stayed but a short time, and it was fortunate for the ship that when both of these were lost the third man on the list, Engine-Room Artificer Leonard Williams, who had been a prisoner of the Japanese, was to prove exceptionally possessed not only of the technical qualities needed to take complete charge of the ship's engines, ably seconded by Engine-Room Artificer Ian McGlashan, but also of those personal qualities of leadership, resourcefulness and devotion that were to earn him the Distinguished Service Medal. He was an exceptional hand — intelligent, quite selfless and a fine messmate and lower-deck leader. His friend McGlashan was a very similar stamp, highly intelligent and of cheerful heart. Another key rating was Chief Petty Officer Stoker Mechanic Owen Aubrey, of Wimborne, a first-class old hand and a delightful party man.

In Stores Petty Officer John McCarthy we meet one of the ship's leading characters. A typical Northern Irishman, with a broad brogue, he was one of those rare and excellent people who have their job absolutely 'taped'. It was his business to have charge of the ship's stores and of the victualling (an office that was to be of special importance and difficulty), and 'if ever there was a halfpenny wrong in his accounts', says the First Lieutenant, 'there was a bombshell'. He was tremendously loyal and, outside his technical duties, was to show himself a splendid lower-deck leader, always to the front in any kind of danger or difficulty.

On the same domestic side of the house was Petty Officer Cook (S) George Griffiths, a Staffordshire man from Hednesford, very thin, said to have formerly been a jockey, who was to have his own special problems in keeping hands fit and contented, with his assistant George Cavill; their standards of feeding the ship's company, reported the RAF medical officer who was oddly to be brought into the business, were 'incomparably better than the usual standards of cooking in the services'. There was also a civilian on the domestic side. This was John Macnamara, the young Naafi canteen manager, short, well-built, dark, amusing, cheerful through all trials as Cockneys so often are, a most effective member of the ship's company and as good a canteen manager as any to be found in the Fleet. During the period of the ship's long trial he was given the duties and status of a petty officer and showed a power of command above the average.

Other outstanding figures of whom we shall see a good deal are Leading Seaman Leslie Frank, who so ably stepped into Nicholls's shoes as coxswain — a thick-set, four-square figure, dark, unruffled, quietly humorous, with twenty-four years' service in the Navy and a flair for getting the best cut of life on board ship; Petty Officer W. H. Freeman, the Gunnery Instructor ('GI'), reserved and intellectual; Electrical Artificer Lionel Chare, plump of figure, sallow and slightly pock-marked of face, a man utterly selfless and sincere, to be burdened with many cares excellently handled; Electrical Mechanic Malachy Donnelly, his chief assistant; Telegraphist J. L. French, the slow-spoken, soft-eyed, thick-browed Devon countryman, a willing horse to whom no journey was too long and by whom Admiral Madden was to be 'filled with admiration'; and last, but by no means least, Able Seaman Jack Walker, the bridge telephone hand, an experienced old salt and a great character, who was privileged to be slightly cheeky to officers, as he frequently was, though always in the best of good humour.

These are a few of the shipmates we shall have in our story. They are important to us, for, whatever else may appear, not least of the forces that bore the ship through her adversities was the firm, confident morale infused by the fine lower-deck leadership of her petty officers.

We shall meet others as we go along. We may note two things — first that they were nearly all very young, few being married, and sixteen being Boy ratings, and secondly that they were a very ordinary ship's company, most of them coming from the city streets that so often produce fine seamen. Though they had excelled at Hong Kong in races for small yachts and at games, they had not yet, otherwise, made for themselves a name as a ship of special excellence. The new hands embarked at Hong Kong, moreover, represented a change in the composition of the ship's alloy, which thus had to be moulded afresh to a firm and positive pattern. *Amethyst*, therefore, had not yet acquired any particular lustre in the eyes of the Fleet; and, after all, was she not the 'canteen ship' of the Far East, the 'tail-end Charlie', the most junior of all?

CHAPTER 3: THE OUTRAGE

THE FRIGATE duly left Holt's Wharf at 8 am on April 19th, stopping to disembark her British pilots off the Woo Sung Forts and to take on two Chinese river pilots. For the Yangtse, with its shifting sandbanks, its numerous islets and its seasonal floodwaters, is at all times difficult to navigate, especially from October to April when the water is very low. The weather that morning was like that of a mild English summer day. The young ship's company, who were still in their blue winter rig, were in great spirits, rather tickled with the idea of seeing someone else's war as spectators and slightly cynical about it all. They numbered some 160 officers, ratings and Chinese.

Shortly after sailing, Skinner learnt by a signal from Donaldson, Naval Attaché in Nanking that the Nationalists would not accept the Communists' extreme surrender terms, and that the armies under General Chu Teh could accordingly be expected to make their attack across the Yangtse on the morning of the 21st, which would give *Amethyst* plenty of time to get safely and quietly to Nanking and *Consort* enough time to get out as far as the quiet anchorage of Kiang Yin.

Uneventfully *Amethyst* steamed up the great river, several miles wide, till at 5 pm she reached Kiang Yin, the point at which the estuary narrows suddenly to the waters of the river proper. As navigation of the Yangtse by night was hazardous, and moreover forbidden by the Chinese Navy, Skinner here asked leave of the Chinese Senior Naval Officer in the *Yat Sen* to anchor, and received the reply: 'You are welcome.' Several Chinese warships were anchored here, including a destroyer and some landing craft. As night came on the Chinese requested Skinner to darken ship, and although he considered that it would be more appropriate for a neutral ship to remain lit, he naturally complied with the request. That night, in the wardroom, the officers played a quiet game of bridge.

Soon after five o'clock on the morning of the 20th, as the sky was beginning to lighten over the flat landscape, *Amethyst* weighed and proceeded slowly up-river in the grey light. Veils of mist hung about the surface of the dusky water and enveloped the frigate as her bows slipped into them. She would comfortably reach Nanking early that afternoon. At 6.30 am she anchored again, one mile north-west of Liu Wei Chiang, on account of fog, but after an hour's wait was able to proceed up-river at slow speed. At eight o'clock, as she neared the troubled area, Skinner gave orders for precautions to be taken. The canvas Union Jacks had already been slung over the ship's sides, port and starboard, ready to be unfurled. Speed was increased to about sixteen knots. Skinner now ordered the first degree of readiness, with the engine-room standing fast, the implication of which was that the engine-room carried on normally but that all other hands went to action stations. The bo'sun's pipe shrilled and all hands moved to their tasks. The awning on the quarterdeck used in tropical waters was left peacefully spread and the guns, though their electrical firing circuits were tested, remained in their visiting-day fore-and-aft positions as evidence of quiet intent. The frigate went steadily on her way. The light had greatly improved, but a slight mist still thinly veiled the landscape.

Half an hour later, about opposite Low Island, or Yung An Chou, where many of the great Yangtse log rafts are broken up, there was a crackle of rifle-fire from the north shore and some small squirts of water splashed up about the ship. A moment later there was a louder shock and a fountain of water shot up near the ship. From the bridge Skinner ordered the director — which by its Barr and Stroud rangefinder, and other instruments high up in the director tower, controlled the fire of the 4-inch guns — to bring the ship's armament to bear on the hostile guns, ready to reply. Battle Ensigns were broken out at the foremast head and the yardarms. The crew of X gun, aft, was ordered to unfurl the Union Jacks that hung ready over the ship's sides. Other shells followed, over and short of the ship, fairly near. Skinner then ordered the gunnery control officer to open fire as soon as he could locate the target, but the mist was a handicap to vision and, as ships so often find when engaging landward targets, nothing could be seen but faint puffs of smoke which it was impossible to fix. *Amethyst*'s guns accordingly remained silent. About a dozen rounds were fired by the Communist battery in fifteen minutes. Fire then ceased, probably because *Amethyst* had passed beyond the battery's arc of fire, and Skinner gave the order 'Hands relax action stations'. No shell had hit the ship.

Skinner, turning to the Yeoman of Signals, remarked with a smile: 'Spoiling Number One's paintwork, Yeoman?'

There was a light-hearted laugh, for the ship's paintwork, which might have been damaged by splinters from the bursts of instantaneous-fused shells, was one of the responsibilities of the First Lieutenant, who was always grumbling about the stinginess of the Treasury. Weston himself, who was responsible for gunnery also, said:

'Don't think I need worry, sir; I call that a first-class example of damned bad shooting.'

'Yes,' answered Skinner, 'you'd think they couldn't possibly have missed. If their other batteries are no better than that, we can all be easy.'

For a land-mounted gun to miss a target of that size at a range of about half a mile certainly showed a gross incompetence. But to have fired on the ship at all had shown a greater ignorance of a more serious sort. Events were to prove that the crude material of which much of the Communist army was made up was ignorant of many of the usages between nations. In particular, they were completely ignorant of ships. Few of them had ever seen one. They did not even recognise the British flag — neither the Union Jack nor the White Ensign. They did not know that the recognised practise of halting a ship among civilised nations was, if not by signal, to fire a round across her bows.

To appreciate what is soon to happen, we may note here that to a land-mounted gun a ship is an unusually large and easy target. Its bulk and height make large allowances for the gun's inherent error. At very short ranges every shot should be a hit, the only drawback of the gun on wheels being that it cannot traverse, or swing laterally, very fast or very far. Moreover, a ship engaging field guns on land is seriously handicapped by two factors: first, as a field gun usually fires from behind the cover of a hill, wood, building or the like, it is often impossible to locate it exactly; and second, in the narrow waters of a river the ship is robbed of her normal freedom to manoeuvre. In a very short time *Amethyst* was to experience these harsh limitations and was to learn that not all the Communist batteries were as incompetent as the first one.

Immediately after this first encounter, Skinner passed a signal down to PO Telegraphist Mewse in the wireless office to several addressees, reporting the event, but the signal was encrypted and, due to later events, never sent. For events now moved with devastating speed. Some forty minutes after the first incident, *Amethyst* was steaming at reduced speed, with the flat Kou An Reach, clustered with trees and occasional homesteads, on her starboard hand and Rose Island, very flat and marshy, to port. The banks of the river were black with wild duck. The weather had now cleared, the sun shone from a blue sky, but a haze still hung over the more distant scene. Besides the White Ensign, *Amethyst* was showing the large Union Jacks over the side. Her quarterdeck awning remained spread. Her guns had not replied to the first assault. She had committed no unfriendly act, nor any uncircumspect one. At about 9.30 pm when all around was entirely peaceful, a shell whipped over the frigate from starboard and plunged into the river. Skinner on the bridge at once ordered full speed ahead and turned the ship away towards the south bank to increase the range of the hostile battery. Observe particularly, that, when Skinner ordered: 'Full ahead both engines' on the voice-pipe to the wheelhouse, both the port and the starboard engine-room telegraphs, manned by Ordinary Seaman Wright and Leading Seaman Frank, were put over to 'full ahead'.

What happened in the course of the next minute or two was so devastating that it is difficult to relate events in their ordered sequence. Four shells, in quick succession, hit three separate and vital parts of the ship in the space of a few seconds, and the interacting consequences of each brought *Amethyst* to the brink of destruction almost in the twinkling of an eye. Geoffrey Weston, the Number One, was forward on B gun-deck when he heard the first shell pass over, and he made at once for the bridge. He had just reached the wheelhouse, from which the coxswain steers the ship, immediately below the bridge, and was about to go through, when a second shell crashed directly into it. The whole ship shook. Weston hurried in and saw the wheelhouse choked with smoke and fumes, and saw also that, of the four men in the wheelhouse, Wright lay seriously wounded in the stomach. Sinnott was badly hit and Nicholls, the coxswain, with multiple wounds in the head and legs, had fallen across the wheel he was manning, dragging it over to port. Leading Seaman Frank, knocked down by blast, recovered, stepped over and took the wheel from him, pulling it back to starboard and trying to call up the bridge on the voice-pipe.

On the bridge, Skinner, seeing the ship going too far to port, at once ordered 'Hard a-starboard,' but her bows were already pointing south towards the shoals of Rose Island. The ship swung still farther round, at speed, her bows heading straight for the shore. Before any of the engine-room staff could appreciate that something was amiss, it was too late to save the situation.

Ignorant of this happening, Weston hurried through the stricken wheelhouse and up to the bridge. Here he found gathered at their respective tasks the Captain, Berger as Navigating Officer, Mirehouse as Action Officer of the Watch, Ordinary Seaman Driscoll, Signalman Roberts and one of the Chinese pilots, very tall and thin. The moment Weston came up on the bridge the Captain turned to him and said: 'Open fire, Number One.' Weston accordingly took the Principal Control Officer's phone from Driscoll, his communications number, and ordered 'Open fire' to the director, where Stewart Hett was stationed as Gunnery Control Officer.

At that precise instant, the words just spoken into the instrument, two direct hits were made on the bridge in rapid succession. Every soul on the front of it was killed or severely wounded. Skinner fell grievously hurt with multiple wounds in the shoulder, side and back, to linger in pain for nearly two days before death. The Chinese pilot was mortally hurt likewise, the back of his head blown off. Berger and Mirehouse were both wounded and unconscious. A splinter took out Roberts's eye. Driscoll, a loyal and faithful man of exemplary behaviour, fell dead at Weston's side. Weston himself was struck by a splinter, 'about the size of a matchbox', that tore through his lower lungs and lodged in his liver.[3]

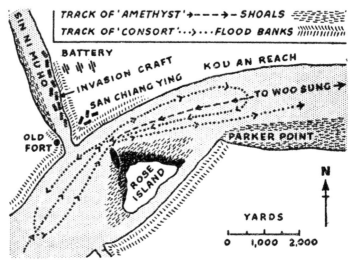

At Rose Island.

Alone of them all, Weston was miraculously conscious and he fought instinctively to take control. As he crouched on the deck of the bridge, coughing blood, with the dead, dying and wounded clustered around him, and the Communists' shells continuing to fall, the ship's extraordinary and sudden peril gradually disclosed itself to his returning senses. He saw her racing at full speed for the shore of Rose Island and tried to con her back into mid-stream, ordering 'Hard a-starboard' on

---

[3] It is still there.

the voice-pipe to the wheelhouse. When this failed to have effect he at once ordered: 'Full astern both engines.'

Down in the wheelhouse, Frank, now the only able hand, with three badly wounded shipmates lying close to him, stepped from the wheel to the port engine-room telegraph and pulled the lever over from 'full-ahead' to 'full astern'. Then he sprang over to the starboard telegraph and attempted to do the like, but it would not move. He tried then to pass the order to the engine-room by the voice-pipe, but could get no answer, for the pipe had been severed. From the bridge he heard Weston call sharply:

'Full astern, cox'n, full astern.'

He answered:

'Wheel's hard a-starboard, sir, but the starboard telegraph is jammed and there's no answer from the engine-room.'

Thus, with the starboard engine still on 'full ahead', the ship was turned still farther to port, and making at speed for the shore of the Island.

Down in the engine-room ERA Graham saw the pointer of the starboard telegraph move right off its scale and he realised what had happened. Wilkinson himself then gave the order for full astern on both engines, but it was too late, and, by an extraordinary combination of mishaps, with her port engine stopped and her starboard engine at full speed, *Amethyst* drove her bows gently, imperceptibly, but very firmly into a mud-bank 150 yards from the western shore of Rose Island — a sitting target for the Communist guns.

Weston thereupon immediately made a 'flash' signal (taking priority over all others in the air) to all ships:

Under heavy fire. Am aground in approx, position 31 degrees 10 minutes North 119 degrees 50 minutes East. Large number of casualties.

This position, as recorded on the telegraphist's pad, was many miles wrong, but the ship was shaking from repeated shell bursts and the chart had been torn to shreds and was covered in blood.

But this was not all. In the same few seconds that all this had occurred *Amethyst* received another crippling blow. Although no one on the bridge yet knew it, another shell had penetrated and wrecked the low-power room below deck, where so much of the ship's electricity was developed, and had killed Electrician's Mate Hicks. The gyro, the wireless, the electric control and firing circuits of guns, the ship's lighting and other services were put out of action. Frank, in the wheelhouse, was the first person to know that this had happened, when the tell-tale red lamp showed him that the gyro was out of action, but at that moment there was no. one on the bridge conscious enough to hear his anxious reports on the voice-pipe.

Simultaneously with all these occurrences and within a few seconds of the hit on the wheelhouse, Hett, in the director-tower, was trying to bring the 4-inch guns on to the target, but with the ship now stern-on to the north bank, and fast by her bows in the mudbank, the two forward guns were unable to bear. Only X gun in the stern could engage. X gun came to the ready and was given the order 'Shoot'. But there was no answer from the gun, for the electric fire-control circuits had also been put out of action by that disastrous shell in the low-power room. Down in the transmitting station, below the wheelhouse, the extinguishment of the indicator lamp told Monaghan what had happened and he immediately passed the order: 'All guns local control quarters firing' and informed the director that he was proceeding to X gun. He hurried out of the transmitting station to find the air filled with the sharp smell of high explosive, a trickle of blood running down the ladder from the wheelhouse and the cries of the wounded coming from all sides. 'The whole upper deck,' he said, 'was an absolute inferno.' All this, which has taken five pages to describe, occurred in less than thirty seconds.

At X gun, the captain of the gun, Leading Seaman J. Mullins, found himself, as captains of guns usually rejoice to do, in independent command of what was left of the ship's armament. He had no clear and distinguishable target, except that the flashes of the hostile battery came from a little north of San Chiang Ying at a range of about 2500 yards. Exposed in the stern to the worst of the Communist fire, he and his twin guns fought a gallant little action, with Monaghan correcting his fire for range. His first casualty was Ordinary Seaman Griffiths, killed by a shell splinter while serving the crew with ammunition. Then, after firing about thirty rounds, said Monaghan in his narrative, 'there was a terrific crash from the starboard side of the gun-shield and I saw four of the gun-crew lying on the deck. Running to the rear of the gun, I saw that a shell had penetrated the armour-plating of the gun-shield, killing the trainer and breech worker and wounding most of the rest.' With five dead or wounded around them, Mullins and the crew of the left gun continued to engage with coolness and determination, until presently the Gunner ordered him to evacuate the gun, with the intent of avoiding further fire being drawn on the ship and so of saving life. For by now the deck of the frigate was so littered with dead and wounded and so splashed with blood that it was difficult for anyone to move about.

Just before this, Weston, having tried all he could to work the ship free of the mud, had stumbled down from the shattered bridge, where he could now serve little purpose, to see for himself what was happening. Passing again through the wrecked wheelhouse, he saw Wright, who in his eyes was the likeness and image of the ideal young sailor, in great pain from his stomach wound. Himself faint, he tried to help Frank, now that the wheel could no longer be served, to carry Wright down the ladder, but he had no strength to take the weight of the seaman's body properly, so that Wright banged his head on the steps, mercifully passing into temporary unconsciousness.

Weston then made his way to the wireless office and made an urgent signal reporting what had occurred, but, as the wrecking of the low-power room had put the wireless out of action, the signal could not be passed. He then came out of the wireless office to see the Communist shells still whipping about the ship. With their instantaneous fuses, they splintered viciously on the steelwork of the ship or detonated on the surface of the river, shooting up plumes of hissing water and black explosive. They were coming at an average rate of two a minute. *Amethyst* was helpless either to fight back or to run away. She was cornered.

Upon the wounded First Lieutenant, who now took command of the ship, there thus devolved a desperate situation. This was a time for a firm grip and a cool head. He called his tall servant, Ordinary Seaman Jack Day, and, leaning on his shoulder, went about the ship, clambering over the dead and wounded. He went aft, saw the quarterdeck awning in ribbons but Mullins firing with determination at X gun. He actually considered putting out in the motorboat with a white flag to the north bank to attempt a parley with the Communists over their unexplainable assault, but found that the motorboat, too, had been hit. He returned to X gun just after Monaghan had ordered it to cease fire and, with the aid of Able Seaman Mulley, put out a small fire on the gun-deck and dragged from the mounting the burning body of one of the crew.

Fearing that the Communists might now attempt to board the ship, he then gave orders for rifles and Bren guns to be distributed and for hands to take station to repel boarders. Hands came up instantly to obey but, when it was seen that several more men were quickly killed or wounded, the order was rightly repealed. Unable to stand for long, and unable to lie down by reason of his wound, Weston then sat down on the deck, panting for breath, and said to himself: 'This is where Weston hands in his chips.' But he continued conscious of the situation, giving his orders to one of the other officers, which they executed. He was acting by swift compulsions, driven by instinct.

Down below, meanwhile (again in the first minute or two), another direct hit had shattered the sick bay, killing Boy Maurice Barnbrook, who lay sick in bed, but miraculously doing no harm to the doctor, Surgeon-Lieutenant Alderton, his Sick Berth Attendant, Thomas Baker, or Macnamara, the canteen manager, whose action station this was. Alderton therefore, together with his staff, quitted the sick bay and went about the ship, administering morphia and first aid, collecting the wounded and carrying them down to the after messdeck. In this dangerous business, with the ship being repeatedly struck and her upper deck sprayed with splinters, Alderton himself, in the words of Berger, was going about with 'an air of cheerful unconcern', and receiving devoted help from Stores PO McCarthy, whose brisk person and North Irish brogue were conspicuous in every dangerous situation throughout the engagement, together with GPO Heath, PO Webb and others of the gunnery staff, who had rescued Skinner from the shattered bridge.

Everywhere Hett's cool head and Strain's busy hands were setting a steadying example and many acts of personal heroism were performed that day — too many, indeed, to have been known or told. When a shell penetrated the depth-charge store, detonating in a box of demolition charges and the room filling with burning TNT, Petty Officer Freeman at once put on a Pattern 230 breathing apparatus, went undismayed into the store and put out the fire, thus saving a dangerous situation and quite probably the ship.

Another shell had made a dangerous waterline hole in the tiller-flat — the half-deck on which the engine that actuates the rudder is situated — and water poured in to a depth of six feet until emergency measures were taken to stop the flow temporarily. The same shell partially wrecked the wardroom wine-store. The lower decks were awash with water from burst water pipes, and severed electrical cables hung everywhere in ragged confusion.

About this time, while on the upper deck near the funnel, Weston, weakened by his exertions, fainted. On the other hand, Berger, wounded in the chest and with all his upper clothes stripped off him by the blast of the shell, had now recovered consciousness and was presently able to move about the ship. He found Weston sitting on deck outside the radar office and asked:

'How are you feeling, Number One?'

Weston replied: 'Fair enough, Pilot. Brain's quite clear. I shall retain command. But if I pass out, be ready to take over.'

Throughout the rest of the action, badly hurt himself, Berger stood-in whenever Weston collapsed. When no longer able to walk he ordered two hands to carry him. It was a little after 10 a.m. and the picture that presented itself to Berger's eyes was enough to have daunted all but the bravest spirits. The crack of shells detonating on the ship's steelwork had the menacing note to which nothing else can be compared. The shattered works, the dead and wounded lying everywhere, the immobility of the ship, the dead wireless, the silent guns, the pungent smell of high explosive and the cries of the injured combined in one threatening spectacle and augury; the ship and her company, it seemed, were being hammered to destruction by a people with whom we were not at war. Yet, in spite of all, the heart of the ship stayed sound and strong and the spirit of her company, who behaved that day like men inspired, remained high and unshaken.

In the ship's helplessness and momentary inaction there was now one thing that called urgently to be done. Some thirty-five or so dead and wounded still lay on the deck where they had been hit. Except forward, it was impossible to move anywhere about the deck without stepping over their bodies, and several were being hit afresh as more shells crashed. Thus Able Seaman Vincent was first wounded by one shell and then killed by another. Accordingly Weston now gave orders for the wounded to be evacuated to Rose Island.

As many as possible were therefore carried aft to the quarterdeck instead of below, together with a portable wireless set so that, when landed, they could maintain contact with the ship. Alderton and Baker, on their way to prepare the wounded for the evacuation, stopped to give Weston an injection of morphia where he sat on the deck. They then went aft to the quarterdeck, but on reaching it a direct hit killed both of them instantaneously. It killed Probationary Writer Tattersall also. By a splinter from the same shell, Mirehouse, already wounded in the leg on the bridge, received another wound in the head. Another shell hit the portable wireless set, spraying the wounded with burning acid, and again Mirehouse was a victim.

Only one boat — the starboard whaler — was seaworthy enough to take the wounded ashore. Hands lowered it coolly and steadily and hauled it round the bows to the less exposed port side. An attempt was made to repair the motorboat, damaged by splinters, but a direct hit on it now put this out of the question. The carley life-saving floats were accordingly slipped.

But was it now a matter of evacuating the wounded only?

The cease-fire by X gun had had no effect on the battery at San Chiang Ying, which still continued its bombardment. The ship was being repeatedly hit, nearly every hit resulting in casualties. Close to Weston a man died drumming the deck with his heels. Another fell near him, struck in the artery that passes through the shoulder. A fountain of blood poured out but no one knew how to apply a tourniquet to that part; his blood drained out over the deck like a river till suddenly, in a death convulsion, he leapt up, ran across the deck and fell down a companion-ladder lifeless.

Having no means, whether by force or signal or mere inaction, of inducing the hostile guns to silence, *Amethyst* had now become a passive and almost helpless target. 'It seemed certain to me,' said Weston, 'that the Communists were bent on bombarding the ship to destruction. There was now no action we could take to prevent it and every minute someone was being killed or wounded.' The chief purpose now, therefore, must be to save lives. Cut off from the outside world, he had to make an agonising decision. Sitting on the deck and speaking with difficulty, he said to Berger:

'Pilot, we shall have to abandon ship temporarily.'

'Abandon, Number One?'

'Evacuate. Until nightfall. Keep a steaming party on board and get a dozen volunteers to help the wounded off. Get the rest ashore under cover till dark. Then bring them back and we'll refloat the ship.'

Berger gave orders accordingly, walking coolly round the ship and ordering 'Swimmers over the side'. There was not a man who was not ready to volunteer to stay for the wounded and Berger was obliged to select from all those who came forward. Again McCarthy was conspicuous and under his cool, brisk direction four wounded, together with fresh water, medical stores and food, were lowered over the side into the whaler, now on the port side. With Monaghan in charge, three volunteers jumped in, manned the oars and pulled for the shore, about one hundred yards away, while the unwounded took lifebelts, jumped over the side and swam or paddled the carley floats by hand to the shore.

Almost every movement in and about the ship, except for a small area on the port side forward, was under close observation from the north shore. Not content with immobilising the ship, or even with the continued bombardment of it, the Communists now turned cold-bloodedly on the men who were evacuating. On the whaler, the rafts and the men in the water they turned not only their artillery but their machine guns and rifles also, like a German submarine machine gunning the men from the ship that it has torpedoed. Able Seaman Sinnot, one of the ship's best athletes, lying wounded in the whaler, hit already in the wheelhouse, was hit again, mortally. Two others were hit in the water and drowned. Aubrey, the laughing GPO Stoker Mechanic, unable to swim, was also drowned or shot, supported till the last possible moment by a gallant shipmate. At 10.45 am, in an effort to stop this barbarity, someone — it is not clear who[4] —

_____

[4] More than one account states that the order was given by Skinner in

ordered a sheet to be hoisted as a white flag, but the Communists took not the slightest notice and continued to rake the shallow waters and the shore. Realising its futility, and fearing also that it might be taken as a sign of surrender and an invitation to board, Berger had the sheet hauled down again.

So hot was the fire, indeed, that Berger quickly appreciated that an even greater loss of life might be incurred in continuing the evacuation than in staying in the ship, and he therefore stopped all further evacuation. The previous order had in any case not reached all in the ship and there were few, if any, who would not have preferred to stay at all costs. Those who went did so because they were ordered.

Some sixty ratings reached Rose Island, together with Wilkinson, the Engineer Officer, who had suffered some nasty wounds about the neck and head but had managed to swim ashore, and six Chinese. Monaghan arrived first in the whaler, which was all but capsized as it reached the shore by a shell that fell close alongside it, throwing the wounded and the crew into the water. Monaghan grabbed the painter and pulled the whaler up the bank, while hands helped the wounded. The swimmers, wounded and unwounded, then began to struggle ashore in small groups, the small-arms fire kicking up little spurts of water or sand around them. Many, before entering the water, had thrown off all but their underclothes and were now all but naked, and were barefoot and hatless.

It had been impossible in the circumstances to execute a properly planned evacuation, but Monaghan, having left a hand in charge of the whaler, did what he could to keep the men together, and as they crawled up through the long grass and the bamboo growing on the bank above high water he ordered

---

one of his periods of consciousness.

them to move inland, spread out and take cover. The ground was extremely flat but fortunately the range for small-arms was now long, and the marksmanship of the Communist riflemen, except for their selected snipers, was always poor. At about eleven o'clock, when all hands both ashore and on board ship were out of sight, the Communist fire ceased.

'The sun,' said Monaghan 'was now getting warm and I lay down on the baked earth in the tall grass and endeavoured to collect my thoughts and determine the next thing to do. If we could sit it out till dark, we could ferry all the ratings back to the ship, and during this wait I could try to find a Chinese Nationalist officer and ask for medical help for the wounded. A further shock awaited me, however, when two ratings approached and said: "Sir, we are in the middle of a minefield; I have just sat on one."' Monaghan rose and inspected the object, and it was soon found that there were mines everywhere. He therefore passed the word to hands to keep to paths and tracks (though it was later found that all the mines appeared to be harmless).

A little to the northward Monghan could see a Nationalist gun position and he began to make towards it, when two Nationalist officers saved him the trouble and came to him. One could speak a little halting English and said to Monaghan that he would have to ask them all to go to a headquarters on the island. All those in the vicinity accordingly moved off behind a guide, but it appears that here the Rose Island party became divided, one party moving off inland with Monaghan and with Ordnance Artificer W. J. Warwick as senior rating; a second, including Wilkinson and Telegraphist French, remaining on the bank; and a third, apparently under orders to make for the cover of the south bank of the island, moving off in that direction under Petty Officer Heath.

Monaghan's party, many of them barefoot and wearing only underclothes, after a long wandering walk through rice fields, arrived at the island headquarters, which was a walled farm, with a system of crude dugouts, and here the Chinese gave the sailors a friendly and hospitable reception, serving them with tea and cakes. Here also Monaghan met a Chinese colonel, who offered to have the ship's wounded ferried to the mainland and taken to a hospital. Accepting this offer thankfully, Monaghan made back under a guide as quickly as possible to the whaler, found a small party of ratings still on the bank and called for volunteers to row back to the ship. By great good fortune one of those present, who immediately volunteered, was Telegraphist French.

Leaving Wilkinson and about eight ratings under cover on the bank, they pulled cautiously for the frigate at about 11.30 am, escaping a fresh burst of machine-gun fire and using the exiguous cover of the ship's port side forward to enter by means of an escape scuttle that led into the Stoker Petty Officers' mess. They brought back with them Sinnott's dead body. Monaghan reported the situation to Weston, and proposed to him that the remaining wounded should be landed after dark for evacuation by the Nationalists and that the shore party should return on board. We shall see how very far those plans were to go astray.

Meanwhile, however, the ship regained one valuable asset. In the evacuation, with all power shut down, all the telegraphists had been ordered ashore. None except French ever came back. He was indeed not merely the only wireless telegraphist now on board but also the only hand trained in any form of signals, except for the wounded Roberts, also shortly to be lost to the ship. His fortunate return and his devoted service were to prove a vital factor in the trying days still to come and were to earn him the Distinguished Service Medal.

When the evacuation party had reached shore and taken cover, the Communist machine guns turned their attention to *Amethyst* herself and began to rake her upper decks with vicious bursts that hammered the steelwork and ricocheted in all directions. Weston ordered the upper deck to be cleared, except for a look-out posted in the shelter of B gun deck-shield, and he himself, still unable to stand, crawled to a sheltered part of the deck. There he was found by Strain and helped to the wireless office, which he made a temporary command post, in order to be available for signals and near the bridge, sitting propped up, unable to rest except by leaning forward on his arms, and unable to eat or drink. On his instructions, in accordance with the standing instructions when a ship is abandoned, Berger ordered all radar and other secret equipment to be destroyed and thrown overboard, and Hett burned all confidential books and papers.

There now remained on board some seventy-six unwounded, twenty-five or so wounded and seventeen dead. The dead still lay where they had been killed. Most of the wounded had been moved to the messdecks where Macnamara brought them chocolates and sweets and where they received what rough and ready first-aid could be given them by unqualified hands; but those lying on the naked quarterdeck, who had been collected there for evacuation, could not be moved without provoking fresh small arms fire from the Communists, and they were left where they were. Except in the cover of the port side forward, no one could move without drawing a hail of bullets. Only the lookout at B gun remained behind the shelter of his shield.

However, it was something that the shelling had stopped. No more material damage was being inflicted, and life and limb were safe when under cover. In spite of their ordeal — for to most of this young ship's company it was their first experience, and a pretty rough one, of action under enemy fire — and in spite of the perilous position of the ship, her company were steady, collected and resilient, responsive to every emergency and prompt to act. The extraordinary casualties among officers and senior ratings in the first seconds of the action could only too easily have spread a contagion of dismay, but none occurred. The examples of Weston and Berger had set the pattern, but indeed the behaviour and spirit of all hands were in the finest naval tradition. Stewart Hett, finding all the manifold duties of a Number One suddenly thrust upon his young shoulders, rose to the occasion with a quiet and cool efficiency, moving everywhere about the ship and giving sterling service. No one, however, could make good the tragic loss of the medical officer and his assistant.

When the evacuation and the shelling stopped, all hands turned urgently to mending the ship's injuries by whatever means they could. She had received, so far, some fifty-odd direct hits, and of these the dangerous shell holes near the waterline were first tackled, particularly those in the tiller-flat and the wardroom. These were plugged with hammocks and bedding, shored up with mess tables and timber. Pumps were hard at work clearing water. A tremendous amount of damage to electrical gear of all sorts had been sustained and the presence on board of George Strain was the most fortunate of chances. Under him, Electrical Artificer Chare and his team worked themselves to a standstill. With the engines shut down, no high power was available and the low-power room was wrecked, but Strain and Chare rigged up an emergency transmitter and someone ran out under fire to rig a temporary aerial, all normal aerials having been shot away. Most of the decks below had been thrown into darkness and the Oldham's emergency lighting worked at only about 60 per cent efficiency, but the electrical party rigged up an extra emergency 24-volt supply for the mess-deck where the wounded lay. There were countless breaks in electric cables from shell splinters, and many lights, ventilators, pumps and other gear were destroyed; there was not enough insulating tape and many of the cable repairs were left bare and 'alive'.

Besides the more dangerous hits, others in the hull had been in the commanding officer's cabin, where the Captain's Chinese steward, But Sai-tin, was slightly wounded, the First Lieutenant's cabin, the radar store, the central store, the asdic office (from which the ship's submarine-detection gear is operated), the forward messdeck, the Chinese mess. There had been direct hits, not only on X gun, but also on the starboard Bofors and the Oerlikon guns; moreover the navigational efficiency of the ship had been seriously impaired by the severe shaking that the compass had received when the ship was hit and by the loss of the gyro.

Subsequent examination by technicians disclosed that the ship had been under fire from guns of various calibres — mainly 4-inch and 3-inch; but a few anti-tank solid shot of small calibre had been fired also, some of which, entering the hull aft, had penetrated far into the ship, piercing several bulkheads and ricocheting in all directions. One unexploded shell of Japanese manufacture was not found until the ship went into dock in England (quickly emptying the ship of all 'dockyard maties') and is now in the museum of the Royal United Service Institute.

Yet, devastating enough though it was, it cannot be said that the Communists' gunnery was good. With the ship enfiladed from stern to stem, virtually every shell should have been a direct hit on some part of the ship if the range had been properly adjusted. Fortunately, the Communist gunners, one of whom we shall meet later on, had got their 'mean point of impact' short, with the result that rather less than one shell in three hit the ship.

More worrying than these mechanical hurts was the condition of the wounded, nearly all of whom were ranked as dangerous or severe cases, and for whom there was now no professional aid. The tubonic ampoules of morphia were being used up rapidly, and the few now remaining were, on Weston's orders, reserved for the more painful cases. Skinner was delirious and was in great pain whenever the relief of morphia wore off. The wounded Chinese pilot, demented with pain, cried out to be shot, and when no one would do so tried to kill himself by swallowing his tongue. Wright, that fine and exemplary young seaman, had died in the arms of a friend, giving last instructions for his little personal things to be sent to his mother. Berger was no longer able to stand and he retired to the wireless office, where Weston was vomiting frequently. There were supplies on board of ICC morphia ampoules for hypodermic administration, but no one knew how to use them.

So, without further incident for three and a half hours, all hands laboured with such materials as they had to repair the frigate's wounds. Soup, tea and bully beef sandwiches were prepared and issued by McCarthy and the cooks. Then, at about 2.30 in the afternoon, after two Nationalist fighter aircraft had flown over, the lookout on B gun reported that a ship was in sight in the distance, approaching at speed from up-river. Monaghan, accompanied by Petty Officer Freeman and Signalman Roberts, went forward to B gun-deck to investigate, and examined the distant small craft long and carefully. Was it *Consort* hurrying down from Nanking in answer to their 'flash' signal of that morning? Through the distant haze it was impossible at first to be sure, but as the slim, small shape moved nearer, the assumption was confirmed and new hope aroused. Weston was informed in the wireless office and said:

'Of course; I ought to have known she'd come at once.'

Signalman Roberts, the only signalman left, a dour, steady man from Caernarvon, in spite of great pain from the loss of his eye, prepared to signal to her by Aldis lamp as soon as she was near enough, and in the wireless office Telegraphist French sat ready to operate on the TCS set.

When *Consort* was about a mile and a half away, it was seen that she herself was in action. Shells were dropping about her and the sharp flashes from her deck showed that her main armament was actively replying.

On hearing *Amethyst*'s 'flash' signal, Robertson, her Captain, had gone at once by jeep to the British Embassy and broken the news to the Ambassador and to Donaldson. He expected, and soon received, orders from Madden to go at once to the assistance of *Amethyst*. He left Nanking at once, taking *Consort* down-river at twenty-nine knots — faster than a ship had ever before travelled the Yangtse. She was flying seven White Ensigns and three Union Jacks. She came under fire somewhere on the Tan Tu Reach and immediately replied. On reaching San Chiang Ying she opened fire with rapid salvoes from her 4.5-inch guns, knocking out three enemy guns by direct hits without serious damage to herself.

Amethyst watched with admiration as the destroyer gave a fine display of shore bombardment, her salvoes throwing up great spurts of earth and smoke right among the enemy guns. When she had neared to about three-quarters of a mile, *Amethyst* spoke to her on the Aldis and they saw her winking in reply to the opening signals. Roberts therefore passed her two signals. The first said: *Urgent medical aid required*, and the second asked her to set up her TCS wireless on 2990 kilocycles, ready to speak to *Amethyst* by radio telephony. No readable reply, however, was received to their signals from *Consort*, nor did the listening French hear any sound from her on the air. The bright sunlight, it was believed, together with the stress of action, impeded *Consort* from reading the flashes of the lamp.

When she was dead astern of *Amethyst* she made a visual signal asking *Amethyst* if her main engines were sound and if it was possible to pass a tow to take her off the mudbank. When informed, Weston said:

'Out of the question. Why risk disabling another ship? Make *Not until enemy guns silenced*. We'll get off by ourselves tonight.'

The destroyer, however, had meanwhile signalled: *Prepare to tow aft*. On receipt of this signal[5] Freeman, Frank and perhaps Mullins also, crawled out on to the open quarterdeck and, although coming under immediate machine-gun fire, courageously ran out a towing wire. By now, however, *Consort* had passed, and she disappeared round the bend of the river. Up till now she had received little injury and, having turned about beyond Rose Island, came back again, determined to silence the enemy guns and take *Amethyst* in tow. Hands on the frigate were spectators of an impressive sight as she came up-

---

[5] According to some accounts this had been done earlier in anticipation.

river, firing all her armament at the north bank and deliberately destroying any guns that could still be seen in action.

She then, however, ran into very serious and unexpected trouble. In the Sin Ni Mu creek, at the head of which San Chiang Ying stood, it happened that the Communists had assembled one of their main concentrations of craft for the assault crossing, full of troops and guns. Perhaps it was for this reason that the San Chiang Ying battery was a particularly aggressive one. Now, as *Consort* came up-river again, the Communists quickly brought out from these craft a quantity of anti-tank guns, mostly of 37-millimetre calibre, concealed them in hedges, and opened very rapid fire on the destroyer at a range of 400 yards. More and more guns were brought out, were handled with great boldness and determination. *Consort* now had exactly the same ill-fortune as *Amethyst* had suffered. Both bridge and wheelhouse were hit, the captain wounded and the coxswain killed. Both A and B guns were put but of action. Moreover, her main steering was disabled and she was obliged to change to emergency steering from aft, from the tiller-flat — a particularly difficult task in narrow waters and at high speed. Under this furious cannonade she passed astern of *Amethyst*, but when half a mile beyond her she turned about and once more steamed down-river and out of sight, still under heavy fire, not to return. She had been, in Madden's words, 'magnificently handled and fought' under trying and unprecedented conditions, and she had suffered eight men killed, thirty wounded and fifty-six direct hits.

Weston, however, apart from the condition of the wounded, was not at all dismayed. Every good seaman prefers to get himself out of his own difficulties and he was quite confident that under cover of darkness he could refloat his ship and get under way. He was determined to fulfil his orders and reach Nanking, now less than seventy miles away, if he possibly could, and he resisted suggestions that he should make downriver. His engines were perfectly sound and, although Hett alone of all the executive officers unwounded, he felt that he had enough strength himself to see the ship through, if all went normally.

It was then a little after three o'clock. An hour later there came a hail from the shore of Rose Island. The ratings left pinned down in the long grass had met the Nationalist soldiers laying tripwire mines and had asked them where the main evacuation party was to be found; but of course the Chinese could not understand. In response to the hail, the unwounded Chinese pilot in the frigate was brought up on deck to shout to the soldiers in their own language, but he said that he could not hear and would go ashore to talk to them. The whaler was manned, with Monaghan again in charge. As they pulled away, someone shouted to the Gunner:

'Make sure that pilot comes back. He's got his bag with him.'

Guided by the two Chinese soldiers, Monaghan went to the local Nationalist headquarters and found, to his consternation, that they had ferried to the mainland not only the wounded who had been evacuated earlier but all the able hands also. He was able to speak to Heath on the Chinese military telephone, and found that he was some four miles inland and that the Nationalists were not prepared to allow the party to go back to the island and to traverse the minefield at night. He therefore ordered Heath to make his way to Shanghai. We shall follow the movements of this party later, but the sad result was that these sixty valuable hands, including several experienced senior ratings, were now lost to the ship — all but two.

The Nationalists, however, generously proposed to Monaghan that they should send a doctor on board with the pilot at eight o'clock, when it would be dark, and offered bearers and transport to take the ship's wounded to hospital if *Amethyst* would land them after dark. 'The colonel,' said Monaghan, 'was willing to stick his neck out for the wounded but dared not take the risk and the responsibility for what might ensue in attempting to bring the others back to the ship.'

At about 7.15 pm, bringing back with him Wilkinson and the nine ratings, the Gunner returned on board in the whaler and reported. Weston would not accept the suggestion that the wounded should be landed and handed over to the Nationalists, for, in the first place, he considered 'their reliability to be low' — which future events were to show was far from being the case — and, in the second place, he expected *Consort* to return after dark — in which expectation also, unfortunately, he was to be proved mistaken.

It was now dark. Eight o'clock came, but no Chinese doctor. And no pilot.

CHAPTER 4: HOPE DEFERRED

AFTER THE sun had gone down *Amethyst* stirred with new life. The night was her friend. The Communist gunners ashore might see her dark outline and shoot but they would not be able to observe and correct the fall of their shells accurately. Nevertheless, the ship was fully darkened against watchful eyes so that all hands could move about freely, though noise, which carries so clearly across water on a quiet night, was kept to a minimum. Hands, now tired and strained, were still struggling all-out to repair damage; and Chare, as Monaghan testifies, 'worked himself to a standstill all day on electrical repairs and then tending the wounded all night.' The seriously wounded were brought down from the quarterdeck to one of the messdecks, where they were inevitably crowded close together with little room to move between them. Most of them had not yet had any medical attention at all, several were delirious and the condition of all was becoming more and more distressing. Their anxious shipmates felt keenly this inability.to help them. The cupboards and drawers of the shattered sick-bay were ransacked, but no one could recognise anything and in their ignorance they searched first for antiseptics instead of dressings, nor did anyone know how to administer morphia now that the invaluable 'monoject' ampoules had all been used.

Weston still sat propped up in a sitting posture in the wireless office, giving his orders in general terms to one of the other officers, who passed them on for execution. He was now able to stand up again, moving about with the help of a walking-stick, but could still take neither food nor drink without being very sick. He was unable to lie down and, when he tried to sleep, could do so only by sitting forward and laying his head on his arms. Berger also was now in bad shape, having to be carried from place to place.

At 7.15 pm the engine-room flashed up. The engine-room telegraph had been repaired, the hole in the tiller flat plugged and the flow of water in the wardroom checked. By 10.30 pm power was on the ship and French had established wireless telegraphy with Hong Kong. Weston thereupon made the following signal to FO2, giving the first accurate situation report to the outside world:

> *Amethyst* still aground on Rose Island. Am attempting to make good vital damage to refloat and proceed to Nanking. 60 approx, of ship's company including 4 wounded are making way to nearest town… Casualties are about 17 dead including doctor and sick berth attendant, 20 seriously wounded including captain.

And a little later he signalled:

> Please make all signals in plain language as confidential books destroyed.

Then, accompanied by Hett and Monaghan, he and Berger were helped up to the wrecked bridge and Weston gave the order: 'Ring on main engines; obey telegraphs,' and began an attempt to refloat the ship. Engines and rudder were worked for about an hour, but the ship's bows still remained gripped fast in the mud. At 11.30 pm he ordered her bows to be lightened by jettisoning heavy weights on the forecastle and fuel oil from the tanks. At one minute to midnight on April 20th the order to the engines to move astern was given again and in sixteen minutes she was free.

With relief and full of new hope, *Amethyst* set course upriver at eight knots with Frank at the wheel; from now until the end of our story he was to be coxswain of the ship. Weston's purpose was to try to get as far as Silver Island, just short of Chinkiang, that night, the risks of navigation forbidding him to go farther. Those risks, however, were already very serious. The winding river was shoal-ridden. There was no pilot. The chart lay in shreds, all beyond the next three miles totally destroyed and what was left obscured by blood. The gyro-compass was out of action. The magnetic compass was faulty and its electric illumination gone. Virtually their only navigational aid was the echo-sounder, which told them automatically the depth of water beneath them. As they got under way an exasperating loss was sustained when the whaler, the only serviceable boat left, which had been secured alongside as it had been impossible to hoist it, broke adrift in the dark before it could be streamed astern and was lost. Unimportant as it might seem, the loss was to prove a severe handicap, for the ship had now no means of communicating with the shore.

A further embarrassment was that the night was fine and clear and the movements of the black silhouette of the ship's hull must have been visible to eyes ashore. At about 1.15 am small-arms fire began to rattle and splash about her. On the bridge Weston held a brief consultation with Berger and Hett as to what should be done. The passage so far had been very trying, not only for those on the bridge, two of them wounded and Berger in a very faint condition, but also for Frank at the wheel. The river was very low and the passage ahead of them would presently narrow. Had the Communists more artillery covering these narrower waters? This doubt, and the fact that that section of the chart had been destroyed, led them to conclude that they would be jeopardising the ship if they pursued their intention that night. *Amethyst* therefore turned about, went back about two miles and anchored in five fathoms five hundred yards from the Nationalist shore at 1.30 am on Thursday, April 21st. There her company, weary in body, but strong in faith and fortitude, enjoyed a little sleep till daybreak, save for those who continued to succour the wounded and those who kept watch over the dark waters and the troubled land.

In the early hours, in reply to Weston's report on the successful re-floating of the ship, Madden signalled:

> Well done. Advise you shift berth if possible at least three miles farther west...

This was just what Weston had done, and forty minutes later there came another cheering signal from Madden, saying that a Sunderland flying-boat would fly in next day with medical aid. Other help was hinted at also. The Admiral had been moved to immediate and energetic action in *Amethyst*'s behalf.

Facts now crowd in upon us from all directions and actions follow fast upon each other. Day and night the air pulses with the tappings of wireless telegraphy. As the faithful French sits at his key, 'scorning sleep', signals fly between *Amethyst*, Hong Kong, Shanghai, Nanking and Whitehall itself. For the nest of wasps into which the frigate had unwittingly thrust her nose had stung admirals, ambassadors and cabinet ministers to instant action. At home, where the Labour Government was in office, Mr Attlee, the Prime Minister, and Viscount Hall, the First Lord of the Admiralty, were greatly concerned. The Foreign Office became immediately involved and the broad, capable figure of Ernest Bevin came upon the scene. Admiral Brind, who, we have noted before, happened to be at home for a strategic study at Greenwich, called at once on the First Sea Lord, Admiral of the Fleet Lord Fraser. A report was drafted by the Admiralty and the Foreign Office jointly for a statement in Parliament, and submitted at a conference to Mr Bevin. Having read it quickly, he said: 'This is quite unnecessarily defensive. We were entirely within our rights. Reduce it to a quarter of an hour's speaking, and put the facts boldly and confidently.'

A few days later the revised statement was made in the House of Commons by the Premier, and by Lord Hall in the Lords. They ridiculed the Communist broadcast which had said that British and Nationalist ships had made a 'combined attack' on their positions, and they emphasised that the root of the problem lay in the Communists' repeated refusal to have any dealings with our accredited diplomatic representatives. Moreover, they pointed out with great effect that, if the Communists had suddenly developed an objection to our ships making passage in the Yangtse — as they knew very well they were doing — all they had to do was to say so to our Consul in Peking.

Mr Attlee entirely supported the action taken by the men on the spot, and accepted full responsibility. In both Houses the Conservative Opposition pressed the Government to explain why there was no aircraft-carrier in the Far East Fleet (there had in fact been one until a few months before), but naval aircraft could have been of little value in that situation.

From now on, throughout our narrative, though we shall see only what is happening on the spot, we are to remember that every step in the destinies of *Amethyst* was being watched and planned at the highest level. The affair had now become a diplomatic one of great consequence and henceforth Admiralty and Foreign Office worked in close association. Day and night the signals flew between Whitehall and China. The nation, indeed the whole Commonwealth and Empire, America and other nations, too, had been deeply stirred. The World's Press was agog. In England the Red Flag was burnt. A Communist leader, who dared to address a meeting in a naval town, was booed from his soap-box with cries of 'Who murdered our sailors?' It needed no spur of public opinion to move the Government to action, yet none of the activity in high quarters was of the slightest avail, every approach and effort being barred by the stone wall of the Communists' cold indifference; and in the end it was the gallant ship herself that, under the watchful direction of the Commander-in-Chief, found the way out.

Ignorant of all this commotion in high places, *Amethyst* herself, though smarting sorely from her stings, and very tired, was quite undismayed and self-reliant. Even on the messdeck, where the seriously wounded lay, there was no groaning or complaint, save from the delirious Chinese pilot, half demented in his agony. Their shipmates did what little they could for them, and Peggy, the Petty Officer Cook's dog, walked among them wagging her tail. Skinner, although in great pain and at one period without morphia, continued to concern himself with the ship's fate in his moments of consciousness.

The outside world had reacted sharply to the news of *Amethyst's* predicament, and practical help was being planned from several sides. From Nanking, as we have seen, *Consort* had gone off at once the day before in the hope of lending her aid. From Shanghai Vice-Admiral Madden, ready in person to go to the rescue, had moved up at once to Kiang Yin in the cruiser *London* (Captain P. G. L. Cazalet, DSO, DSG) and was joined by *Black Swan* (Captain A. D. H. Jay, DSO, DSC). He was closely considering the various courses open to him to rescue the frigate. He would have liked to send *Black Swan* up by night, but she would have had to hug the Nationalist shore against their ban on night movement, and would have been committing a breach of faith as well as risking serious damage. He considered also reaching *Amethyst* by an expedition of ships' boats by means of the creek (the Hsiao Ho) dividing the island of Tai Ping from the mainland, but this, a twelve hour passage, could have rescued only the wounded and not the ship. Offensive air action was ruled out as there were no strike aircraft nearer than Malaya. Diplomatic action was a course obviously to be considered and he obtained confirmation from Stevenson that this was being attempted, but was warned that, if any agreement at all could be obtained, it would take several days. But 'it was unthinkable', said Madden, 'that those in urgent distress in *Amethyst* should be left without any assistance'. Now that the frigate was refloated and would not need a tow, it would be sufficient to provide her with an escort down-river. He decided, therefore, that the attempt must be made by day with all the force that he had immediately available.

Meanwhile he had made arrangements for emergency medical aid. And far away at Kai Tak airfield, opposite Hong Kong, the RAF had responded at once to the call for help that Madden had made to the Air Officer Commanding. At 10.45 night before, at Madden's request, while *Amethyst* had been struggling to free herself from the mud, Group Captain J. M. Jefferson, the Station Commander, had ordered 88 Squadron to have a Sunderland flying-boat standing by for the 750 miles flight, prepared to drop medical supplies or to land alongside the frigate if possible. Aircraft D-88 was detailed, and during the night the squadron worked to get her fully armed and loaded with medical supplies for dropping.

At 7.25 am on the 21st she was airborne, piloted by Flight-Lieutenant K. H. F. Letford, DSO, DFC, and carrying Group Captain Jefferson and two doctors — Flight Lieutenant M. E. Fearnley, and Surgeon-Lieutenant D. D. D. Morgan, RN — together with two soldiers trained in dropping supplies by parachute. When nearly at the Yangtse, however, she received an operational priority signal from the *London* warning her of heavy gunfire near *Amethyst*, and instructing her to go to Shanghai to await orders.

For even *London* herself, 10,000 tons cruiser though she was, was now in serious trouble. At 9.30 that morning Madden had made a signal to *Amethyst* saying that he was coming at once to escort her down-stream and that she was to be ready to move at 11.30 am. Soon afterwards he sailed from Kiang Yin in *London* through the winding waters, accompanied by *Black Swan*. In a very short time, however, he found himself affronted by the same ruffianly behaviour as *Amethyst* had suffered. In spite of their peaceful purpose, the Communists opened concentrated fire on the two ships from batteries first near Bate Point and then south of Beaver Island, to such effect that *London* was very soon holed in several places, with fifteen men killed and twenty wounded. She replied with her 8-inch and 4-inch guns and with Commander R. G. W. Hare standing up at her compass under fire on the shell-shattered bridge conning her at high speed in dangerous waters; but it was a startling demonstration of the vulnerability of a ship to land artillery at short range, and of the heavy casualties caused by the multiple fragmentations from the impact of instantaneous fuses on steel. She was, of course, a very large target; the worst possible gunners could not have missed her.

It was now Madden's turn to be faced with a distressing decision. He knew that it would be wrong to imperil so valuable a ship as the cruiser and her accompanying frigate and, if this was to be the Communist attitude, he must not go on. We were not at war with them. 'We should have lost,' he said, 'more than we could have gained.'

Reluctantly he gave the order for his little force to turn down-river again and he signalled to Weston:

> Am sorry we cannot help you today. We shall keep on trying. Stay where you are for the present unless forced to move, in this case go upstream. Further instructions will follow.

Repugnant though it was, it was entirely the right decision to make. Political issues also would become deeply involved. Madden therefore now made a signal to the Commander-in-Chief at home, repeated to the Admiralty and others, urging that steps should be taken 'at the highest level' to secure some agreement with the Communists for resolving the whole preposterous affair. That meant, of course, diplomatic action, with responsibility at Cabinet level, if such action was possible with a revolutionary army that had hitherto refused to negotiate with foreign diplomatic or consular representatives. We shall see presently that attempts were made immediately. Madden, however, until the return of the Commander-in-Chief from England, continued to watch every move on the chart, to examine every possible course for the ship's rescue and to maintain her crew in good heart. He was now back at the mouth of the Yangtse and *Amethyst* filled all his thoughts.

On board the frigate, which had moved out into midstream with steam up ready to accompany her rescuers (only to be shot at again), the gunfire had been plainly heard, and the news from the *London* was a blow to all. They had all been tremendously cheered when, at about 9.30 that morning, they had been mustered on the after messdeck and had been told by Weston of the promised relief. In spite of their predicament, the spirits of all on board had until now remained astonishingly high. Their minds turned always to positive action. As they listened to the sound of the distant guns they were all saying: 'Here she comes! Here she comes!' But when *London*'s signal was received, 'the spirits of everyone', said Monaghan, 'reached an all-time low'. All things seemed to conspire against them. *Consort* had failed, *London* had failed, the promised Sunderland had not arrived. Seventeen dead bodies awaited burial and the condition of the wounded was getting more and more distressing. Their captain lay prostrate. They had no doctor, no boats, no chart and were some sixty hands short. The ship was littered with splinters, broken glass and debris of all sorts, and her upper decks splashed everywhere with blood. Berger, after remaining on duty for twenty-four hours with the greatest fortitude, had collapsed. Weston, between his intervals of faintness, was able to stand and walk for short periods with the help of his stick and could now drink, but could still eat nothing and was breathing with difficulty. Wilkinson somehow remained on duty, his engines reverted to short notice, but Strain, Hett and Monaghan alone were fully able-bodied among the officers.

There was one source, however, from which Weston, had he been able to forecast events, could have accepted help readily offered — the Chinese Nationalists. That morning he received no fewer than three offers from them — twice from army officers who came out by sampan and once from a tall, smart young sub-lieutenant in command of an ex-American landing craft, whom we shall meet again. Weston, ordering Day to dress him in clean uniform, received them all but declined their offers — first because of the Sunderland's expected arrival and later because of *London*'s.

After the failure of the rescue attempt, *Amethyst* spent an uncomfortable few hours. The dead were collected by a party of volunteers, laid out on the quarterdeck and covered with the remains of the awning. The air was agog with the mutterings of wireless telegraphy and the unsleeping French was kept busy — passing a signal asking *London* for instructions on the use of morphia sulphate, taking and answering signals on the possibility of the Sunderland making another attempt to come to them, and listening to signals between higher quarters. All on board knew now that as much as possible of heaven and earth was being moved on their behalf and that the little ship, caught between two rival armies, had now become headline news for the world. For, besides the Admiralty announcements, there was a Reuter correspondent at the Nationalist Army headquarters hard by the *Amethyst*, and he let little pass of so splendid a 'story'.

Soon after one o'clock there was another visit from the Nationalists ashore. They seemed determined to help if they could in spite of the repeated refusals of Weston, who had little faith in them. The Nationalists' attitude was all the more surprising and impressive in that they knew that their enemies across the river were poised for the attack, and one would have expected that they could spare little time and effort to help the British. Yet we shall see to what extremes they were prepared to go in the hour of their own danger and how very sharply their bearing was to contrast with that of the Communists.

What was now proposed to Weston was that someone from the ship should go ashore to discuss with the local military headquarters how medical help should be given to the ship. To this Weston agreed and he detailed Monaghan for the duty.

The Gunner accordingly went off in a sampan, accompanied by a Chinese steward as interpreter and taking a supply of Chinese money with him. He went up-river for about two miles and there was taken to a military headquarters to which was attached some sort of casualty station or small hospital. Here he was given a supply of bandages, splints and so on, and gladly accepted the offer of a Chinese military doctor to come out to the ship. More important still, the local military commander offered to land all the wounded, transport them over the hills by horse and cart, and have them taken to a place of safety. 'I thought,' said Monaghan, 'that it was mighty fine of him, placed as he was, and said so, but he only smiled and said: "It is nothing."' It is quite likely that this headquarters was that of the battalion on the creek called the Hsiao Ho[6] where Kerans was to find himself that same exhausting and frustrating night.

Very relieved, Monaghan returned to the ship at 3.30 pm, bringing with him the Chinese doctor and two medical orderlies. He was a little, slight fellow, this doctor, by name Lieutenant Chu Wei, a qualified doctor, unlike many other medical men in Chinese units; and although he had no morphia, penicillin or other drugs, but only wound dressings, he and his two orderlies did wonderful work and *Amethyst* was to have much cause to be grateful to him.

Weston was now at last persuaded to the course that he had long resisted — that the wounded should be taken ashore and entrusted to the Nationalists. Apart from his more specific objections, which we have already noted, it was only too likely that, if the Communists made their expected crossing that night, the wounded would fall into their hands. There now

---

[6] Hsiao — small; Ho — stream. Pronounced approximately 'Shiaow Ho'. (*Ch'ang Chiang Pilot.*)

seemed no alternative, however, if their lives were to be saved. He accepted Dr Chu's assurance that the casualties would be sent straight to hospital and that he would get Reuter's correspondent to telephone news of their dispatch to the British Embassy in Nanking. The Gunner, who had all along advised this course, was now to go ashore again to make the detailed evacuation arrangements.

No sooner had these plans been made, and Monaghan about to step into the Nationalists' sampan, than those on deck heard the sound of aircraft in the distance eastwards. It was the Sunderland at last, for Weston knew, from a further signal from FO2, that she was going to make a second attempt.

While waiting at Shanghai, Jefferson in the Sunderland had heard from *London* how serious the situation was, and had responded once more to Madden's renewed request for help. The aircraft took off from the Whang Poo river at 3.30 pm, piloted again by Letford, and in an hour sighted the *Amethyst*. Making a low approach, she saw no signs of hostile action and, after a further run past the ship, alighted, taxied close to the frigate, stopped engines fifty yards from the ship's stern and put out her anchor. Monaghan, instead of making for the shore, ordered the sampan men to take him at once to the flying-boat, climbed inboard to explain the situation and to help disembark. They exchanged pleasantries. Fearnley, the RAF doctor, jumped into the sampan with his gear, and at that moment the Communist guns opened fire, a salvo landing in the water a bare hundred yards away.

'They're pretty accurate,' Monaghan said calmly. Before the naval doctor or Monaghan could join Fearnley or discharge their medical stores, the two frightened boatmen of the sampan had made off, heading for the shore, till Fearnley himself seized the oar and made to turn the boat towards the ship; but he rocked it so badly that the sampan men decided that it was safer to risk the shells and obediently took him to the ship.[7] The Sunderland, forced to take off at once, taxied down-tide and down-wind, still under fire and carrying the astonished, bewildered and very chagrined Gunner with her. Another valuable hand was lost to the ship, for Monaghan's resource and initiative had been invaluable throughout.

On the other hand, *Amethyst* had gained a doctor, of whom she was in such desperate need and, although everyone was naturally astonished to see an RAF officer come on board, literally dropped from the skies, no one was ever more welcome. His arrival could hardly have been more unceremonious, for, as he was hauled hastily on board, a shell pitched not far away and he found himself spreadeagled on deck. Young, dark and soft-eyed, Fearnley, who was to prove himself a sterling member of the ship's company in the course of his long and extraordinary stay, had an amusing meeting with Weston.

'Well, always glad to see the RAF,' said Weston as heartily as he could, 'but hasn't the Navy any more doctors?'

'There *was* one,' Fearnley replied, 'but he's gone off again with the RAF! You nearly didn't have me either.'

'I saw you did your best to put yourself in the drink.'

'It wasn't that, but the blighters nearly had me put in the bag by the Communists.'

Weston laughed weakly. 'Oh, I see. I suppose you didn't know which bank was which? As a matter of fact, this is the Nationalist side. *That*' — as the ship shuddered from another hit on the starboard side — 'is the Communist!'

---

[7] Fearnley did not, as sometimes stated, threaten the boatmen with the revolver that Monaghan had left behind.

The Sunderland having got away safely, the Communists switched their fire to the *Amethyst* once more. Not many shells were fired, however, but again she was hit several times — twice more on the bridge, in the wardroom again, in No 7 oil fuel tank and in the starboard turbo-generator room, where the generator was undamaged but where the room began to flood from the burst fire main pipes. No serious damage was done, but the confusion and discomfort were increased and there was more repair work for tired hands.

Why was the Communist artillery behaving in this peculiar way? Weston asked himself. When the ship was aground off Rose Island and the guns seemed intent on shelling the ship to destruction, they suddenly stopped. When, this Thursday morning, she weighed anchor and moved out into mid-river to await *London*, she was shelled again until she moved back, and was then left alone. And now, after the departure of the Sunderland, the shooting once more started and stopped suddenly. It began to look, Weston thought, as though the rebels had now no desire to destroy the ship, but to keep her pinned down until they had made their crossing of the Yangtse that night, when they would be able, they hoped, to seize the ship themselves. So the situation might be read. It was, at least, quite clear that they did not intend to let her slip. The truth of this supposition and the very peculiar reason for it, to be appreciated only by a study of the Communists' own tortuous minds, will presently appear.

Down below in the engine-room, ERA Williams, with excellent foresight and intuition, had, on his own initiative, come to immediate notice for steam as soon as he heard the first salvo directed at the Sunderland. His judgment was right, for after this new attack and fresh damage Weston weighed anchor again. There was no point in sitting still to be shot at.

The important thing now was to go somewhere where the wounded could be peacefully dealt with and safely landed. Fearnley was very anxious that they should be got ashore. Weston therefore made for the Hsiao Ho, in which he would be out of observation from at least the troublesome San Chiang Ying battery, but he found that the water was too shallow and re-anchored in the mouth of it in four fathoms.

Here the two doctors, British and Chinese, worked at their task. Fearnley, who had not before been on anything in the nature of a battlefield, was shocked by what met his eye when he came on board. 'It was,' he said, 'like a front-line dressing station.' He found the wounded crowded close together and their condition was 'lamentable'. Nearly all, he saw at once, would require operations under anaesthesia, some would require amputations and one or two were 'certain to die'. Besides this, he saw seventeen corpses not yet prepared for burial, twisted metal and shattered glass littering the whole ship, water swilling the lower decks from burst waterpipes, all 'heads' (latrines) blocked, his sick bay wrecked, parts of the ship still in darkness, all officers' quarters and the wardroom uninhabitable, and the ship's company tired out. Their morale 'was now being noticeably affected by the presence of the dead and the condition of the dying. The rest of the ship's company had been living with the wounded for two days and a night and were beginning to show signs of strain'. He found also a woeful ignorance of first aid. No one understood that the prime necessity was not antiseptics, but exclusion of air. Nevertheless, many of the ship's company, in their anxiety to help their shipmates, had 'worked with laudable calm and displayed common sense'.

Fearnley, who was full of praise for Chu and his dressers, had brought with him and now administered some blood plasma and the drugs most needed, especially morphia and penicillin. Presently Chu went ashore to give effect to the evacuation plan. He came back at 9.30 pm with four or five sampans and the evacuation began — a slow and difficult business, for nearly all were stretcher cases that had to be manoeuvred over the ship's side in the dark. A few hands who had only slight wounds remained on board; one of these, with a shell splinter in his cheek, was Stores Assistant Brynley Howell. He was about to be sent ashore, but at his own request was allowed by Fearnley to stay on board; and he became, in fact, Fearnley's Sick Berth Attendant and soon proved himself extremely useful.

Fearnley had, of course, fully intended that Weston should go with the rest. He had probed the wound and had treated him with penicillin. When the evacuation began the First Lieutenant was under morphia and asleep, head down on his folded arms on a suitcase on top of the wireless office desk, but on being woken up and told to get ready to go ashore he swore that he would do nothing of the sort.

'I can't possibly leave the ship until I can be relieved,' he said firmly. 'Out of the question. There'd be only one executive officer left.'

'You really ought to go,' urged the anxious young doctor. 'If that wound turns septic, you will have a very serious abscess.'

'Well, I shall have to take a chance on that. Couldn't you take the thing out here?'

'I'm afraid that's quite impossible!'

'Well, anyhow,' said the First Lieutenant obstinately, 'I'm not going.'

Wilkinson, before he himself left, and Hett also added their urgings to Fearnley's, and someone suggested that the doctor should put Weston to sleep, but this he naturally refused to do.

Presently Walker came and reported that the last sampan had gone.

'In that case,' said Weston, 'the question is a purely academic one.'

He gave the order to weigh anchor and at 1.10 in the morning of Friday, April 22nd, the frigate, a dim black shape in the cloud-grey night, moved slowly up-river. No one saw the faint flicker of a torch winking an urgent summons to them from the shore.

Quite unknown to them, undisclosed by sight or sound or signal, help stood expectantly on the reedy shore, trying desperately to reach out its hand to them across the dark. By a bare few minutes she slipped away from the reach of the friendly hand and crept forward on her determined course, stealthily and alone.

CHAPTER 5: THE NIGHT MARCH

FOR IT was not only by air and by water that hands were trying urgently to reach them in their adversity. By land also a little rescue team was struggling to get through, bedevilled by faulty information, vile roads, false directions and all those vague shapes and misty confusions that make up the 'fog of war' with which the soldier on land is only too familiar. To these elements were added the unease and tension of an army about to take flight before the moment of the enemy's onslaught and, in the absence of their own resources, the complete dependence of the rescue party upon that threatened army. It is to the lasting credit of the Chinese Nationalists that, at this crisis of their own destinies, they held out both hands to help a humanitarian cause.

The efforts of this determined little band, in which three nationalities took part, form a vital part of our story, and in order to tell it we must for a moment leave the *Amethyst* creeping cautiously through the night and transfer ourselves in thought to Nanking.

Here, as we have seen, Robertson, on receiving *Amethyst*'s 'flash' signal on the morning of the 20th, had hurried to the Embassy with the startling news before steaming off at speed in *Consort*. When this same news was announced at the normal Embassy staff conference that took place a little later, it was greeted with a sudden hush. Such a thing was unheard of, unthought of, scarcely to be credited. You could, said one of those who were there, have heard a pin fall. But there was nothing that could be done and they must put their faith in *Consort*. There was no means of making representations to the

Communists, for the Communists remained icily aloof, still leaving all embassies marooned in a sea of indifference. About midday came *Amethyst*'s undated signal reporting that she was still under fire and aground, but nothing could be done but await the fortunes of *Consort*.

During the afternoon there came more distressing news, brought unexpectedly by an American diplomatic aircraft (*not* attacked by the Communists) that had recently landed. She had seen *Consort* in action — 'flat out and firing everything she had' — and had watched the progress of events. The aircrew had taken photographs, which showed *Amethyst* aground, and showed, too, the positions of Communist batteries. This news, which was quickly passed to the British Embassy, was the first intelligence that *Consort*'s mission had failed. The concern grew more profound. Donaldson and the small staff of Embassy telegraphists became deeply immersed as the signals crowded the air.

The astonishment was no less when the news spread to other embassies and to the trading communities. All were momentarily stunned. To have attacked a foreign neutral warship, and in waters where rights had been so long recognised by all parties, appeared to people, Chinese as well as Europeans, to be as shocking as an affront to the Ark of the Covenant. Here was a rude and near reminder that the people with whom they would soon have to come in contact recognised no sanctities, venerated no traditions and wore no gloves upon their rough hands.

That night the Commander-in-Chief of the Chinese Navy, Admiral Kwei Yung-ching, that forceful soldier turned sailor, and Madame Kwei gave a small dinner party for seven or eight guests. There were the usual sixteen or so courses. The Chinese Navy provided a lively orchestra by bombarding the

Communist positions, seemingly in breach of the truce, and in consequence the lights kept going out under the vibrations of the cannonade. The meal was further interrupted constantly by telephone calls, causing the Admiral to miss a large number of courses. The calls were mainly from Chinkiang and several of them related to *Amethyst* and to reports, of a confused and uncertain nature, of the landing of her wounded (which had not yet, in fact, taken place). The Admiral was full of apologies to his guests, but the news was important and the telephone of regrettable antiquity.

One of those invited to this party had been Donaldson, but he was that day far too seriously occupied and the Admiral and Madame Kwei had asked the Assistant Naval Attaché, Lieutenant-Commander Kerans, to come in his place. Thus there appears, but at first in a minor role only, the man whom chance was to cast for the central part in all the remaining scenes of this stirring play.

John Simon Kerans was an officer of thirty-three years of age, married and with a young daughter. He came of an Army family — his father in the Worcestershire Regiment and his uncle in the Indian Medical Service, both DSOS; his brother, also in the Worcesters, had been killed in the assault on Keren in Wavell's brilliant campaign against the Italians in Abyssinia. In person Kerans was somewhat tall, fair, slender and spare in figure, what one might call fore-and-aft rigged — the figure one might expect in a man keen on running and fencing, though he played rugger, too. He was long-faced and long-headed in both senses of the term, more interested in facts and ideas and plans than in people, accustomed from long training in Intelligence to assessing information and forming a judgment on it. He was to have acute need of that judgment. Perhaps on account of the same training, he could be exceedingly 'cagey', when necessary, his mind hidden behind a curtain of reserve, and this characteristic we shall observe very positively at work. Withal he had a sense of humour, a taste for classical music and a sharp temper on occasion.

Kerans had entered the Navy through Dartmouth and had served in large and small ships in various waters. The greater part of his war service, however, had been in the Mediterranean, much of the time on the Malta convoys, in one of which the convoy and escort had endured and fought 287 enemy bomber sorties; in 1942 he had gone down in HMS *Naiad* when, wearing the flag of Rear-Admiral Philip Vian and under the command of Captain G. G. Grantham, she had been sunk by a German submarine after an all-day air attack north-west of Solium. Soon after that came his first command, HMS *Blackmore*.

More important for us, however, is the fact that, out of his sixteen years' commissioned service up till 1949, he had spent some seven years or more in Far East waters, from Singapore to Japan, sometimes afloat and sometimes on Intelligence work, and dating back to his days as a midshipman in HMS *Cornwall* in 1934. He had been on the China Station during the bad days of the Sino-Japanese war, and had been at Nanking soon after its ghastly sack by the Japanese, serving in the guard-ship there (HMS *Ladybird*) at a time of great tension and strain, when the presence of our guard-ship had proved of great value and when preparations had been made for the evacuation of British nationals. Just before he came back to Nanking early in 1949 he had been employed on special intelligence duties.

He was also accustomed to, and unaccountably enjoyed, Chinese sixteen-course dinners. On the occasion of Admiral Kwei's dinner on the night of the 20th, however, he, like the

Admiral, had little opportunity or reason to enjoy his meal and he returned to the Embassy very anxious. There the Ambassador presently held a conference with Donaldson, Kerans and the Acting Military Attaché, Major R. V. Dewar-Durie. According to the information that had been received, some twenty wounded from the *Amethyst* had been landed and were being sent by the Nationalists to hospital in Chinkiang. The information was somewhat vague and uncertain, and Stevenson therefore decided to send Kerans off to Chinkiang first thing next morning to investigate the report and ensure the well-being of the men. Then, turning to Dewar-Durie, he said: 'D.-D., you know the language; you had better go along, too.'

Thus we meet another character who is to play a part in this strange affair and who was to be Kerans's close companion for a brief spell. Raymond Dewar-Durie, of the Argyll and Sutherland Highlanders, was some ten years older than Kerans. Inevitably known to all as 'D.-D.', he was of medium height, athletic build and a cheerful disposition. He had spent many years in China and spoke fluently her difficult language. When Shanghai had been occupied by the Japanese in 1941 he, together with Major Sidney Hunt, had made a remarkable escape, which is a story in itself that may one day be told, getting away audaciously in the boot of a Japanese colonel's car and journeying some 1500 miles across China in civilian guise to rejoin allied forces at Chungking. D.-D.'s long stay in China, however, had not suppressed his ardour for cricket and tennis. He was good company and everyone liked him.

These two officers Donaldson duly briefed that night, ready to leave next morning. In case he should be able to make his way to the ship, Kerans was told to obtain a supply of the medical stores that *Amethyst* needed so desperately, and D.-D., knowing his China, supplied himself liberally with Chinese money from the Embassy. More important than either of these commodities, however, Donaldson obtained from Admiral Kwei Yung-chin a letter in which he commanded all concerned to give the British officers the utmost help in their power. There remained only the problem of transport, with which the Embassy was not well equipped, until the Australian Military Attaché, Colonel Alister Clark, appeared and said: 'Better take my jeep.'

So, at 10 am on Thursday, while *Amethyst* was waiting expectantly for HMS *London* a mile and a half south-west of Rose Island, they set out for Chinkiang, the naval and army officers, in an Australian jeep with a Chinese driver. D.-D. was in battledress, and Kerans, with no inkling of what lay in store for him, had nothing but the blue winter uniform that he stood up in and a Burberry. They had not moved a hundred yards before the jeep, of early vintage, broke down. 'None of us,' said D.-D., 'really knew what was the matter with it, but we gave it a good shaking and it worked again.'

Three hours of jolting over a potholed road, erupting into clouds of dust, took them to Chinkiang, an ancient walled city, of which we shall see a great deal, set in a half-circle of hills, some hundreds of yards back from the banks of the Yangtse, but with a modern overflow that contained the old British Concession stretching down to the river. Once a thriving Treaty Port, with a conspicuous British Consulate set on a hill, it had fallen into decay since the departure of those who had built its prosperity, and it now presented to the eyes of the two British officers the sad spectacle of a weary old city from which the inhabitants were beginning to flee before the Communist terror, but on the outskirts of which, clinging to its walls like green-fly to a succulent plant, a swarm of unhappy refugees from the north led a miserable and insanitary life under the exiguous shelter of huts made from straw matting. It was still thronged, however, with Nationalist soldiers, in their drab, olive-green cotton uniforms, their puttees, and their skiing caps, padding noiselessly in their soft-soled cotton shoes along the cobbled streets, and with the neglected wounded hobbling about, unnoticed by a people who look upon the hurts of others with a cool detachment. There was little evidence of imminent battle, nor indeed was there much visible evidence that the Nationalist armies had resolved to adopt the famous counsel of Taoism — that, 'of all the thirty-six alternatives, running away is the best'. Beneath their 'famous Chinese apathy', they seemed cheerful enough as they turned interested and curious eyes to look at the unfamiliar figures in the British jeep.

Kerans and D.-D. made for the sector headquarters of the Chinese Navy, a big, grey, brick house near the river front, and there they saw the Chief of Staff, Captain 'Mark' Meh, a British-trained officer who spoke English well. He was small, dapper and lively, very much on our side, and was to prove a great friend. In answer to Kerans, he said that the reported arrival in Chinkiang of twenty British wounded had no truth in it, but he gave the fresh news that Heath's Rose Island party of about sixty had that morning safely left Wutsin by train for Shanghai. Kerans then asked Meh if he would place a craft at their disposal, so that he could take the medical supplies that he had for *Amethyst*.

'I am very sorry,' said Meh, 'but we should find that very difficult. The few craft that we have left here have been knocked about a good deal. You would almost certainly get shot up and we can't afford to lose any more of our craft.'

Kerans was nonplussed. He and D.-D. retired to a small sideroom off Meh's office and were disconsolately eating a dish of noodles, when there came into Meh's office the smart young Chinese sub-lieutenant whom we saw taking his landing craft to the *Amethyst* to offer help. Meh at once called in the British officers and the young sub-lieutenant told them with precision and authority what he knew, which, although it was little, was definite and important. From him Kerans learnt that the wounded were still on board, that the ship was afloat and apparently seaworthy, and — what was specially important — that she was now anchored off Tai Ping Island. He added that he had been himself fired on by the Communists but had escaped unhurt.

All this was valuable news, but it was very trying to Kerans that he could not reach the ship, some seventeen miles downriver. He therefore made tremulous contact with Nanking on the antique telephone — one of those veterans that incorporates a ringing handle — and reported to Donaldson.

'There doesn't seem to be anything you can do,' said Donaldson, 'so you'd better come back.' A little later, however, he rang back to tell Kerans that he must do his utmost to reach *Amethyst* before dark by whatever means he could. Having received a signal from Weston, he confirmed the young Chinese officer's information about the ship's new position and added:

'She is certain to try to move farther upstream tonight, so you must get to her before dark. But you will have to hang on where you are for a bit, as the American Embassy are lending us a doctor and he is on his way now. Lieutenant-Commander J. W. Packard, US Navy. He should be with you in an hour or so.'

This very welcome new help had been due to the kindness of the American Ambassador, Dr Leighton Stuart. He had rung up Stevenson that morning to express his sympathy and had asked: 'Is there anything we can do to help?' And when Stevenson had told him the need for medical help, he had said that he would send Packard right away.

Kerans put his new problem to Meh. 'I have got to get to the ship somehow,' he said. 'If you can't spare a craft to go by river, we shall have to go by land. We shall need trucks for the wounded, a guide and that sort of thing.'

'I'll do what I can. You realise, of course, that we are expecting the enemy to cross any time now? Things are a little precarious.'

'I realise that fully, and that we are asking you a great deal.'

Meh was a staff officer much above the average, well fitted to deal with a confused situation. He was, of course, profoundly impressed by the letter from Admiral Kwei that Kerans carried, and he saw that the best way to help now was to get the same kind of high-level authority from the Army. After some more manipulation of the ancient telephone, he was able to tell Kerans:

'I have spoken to headquarters of 4th Army, and General Wang Tso-hua is personally signing a chit instructing all concerned to help you through. They will also let you have a couple of trucks and guides. You'll have to make first for the headquarters of the regiment covering that sector, near Ta Chiang, where everything will be laid on.'

'That's splendid. I'm most grateful.'

'Well, I'd rather like to be in on this myself, too. Mind if I come with you?'

'Wonderful! We should be delighted.'

This was promising. Armed with letters from both Admiral Kwei and General Wang, and with the Naval Chief of Staff in person — a quite extraordinary thing for one in his position — they ought to be able to get anywhere.

At 3.30 pm a large American car arrived, bringing Packard, the US Navy doctor, a big burly figure in a fur-collared windproof jacket, and his Pharmacist's Mate, dark, rotund and Italianate. Three-quarters of an hour later, having collected all the information that they could about the military situation, roads and ferries, they set out, a truly international party of Americans, British and Chinese — with an Australian jeep. Kerans, D.-D. and Meh were in the jeep, Packard and his assistant in the big car, and with them were the two trucks loaned by the headquarters of 4th Army.

Under the mild April sun they drove out of Chinkiang by an earth road and then by a route that took them by the southern fringe of the hills that ranged parallel with the Yangtse. It was the front of the 59th Division. The country here was low-lying and marshy among paddy fields and young cotton, groves of bamboo or mulberry, with occasional tree-shrouded shrines, clusters of dun, mud-walled houses, where the pigs squealed and the small hens scratched, and groups of patient, blue-clad peasants stooping to their tasks or looking up curiously as the 'big-nose foreigners', now so rarely seen, jolted on their way. Pheasants flew from copse to copse and wild duck fed in the innumerable waterways. The road soon became a nightmare of loose stones and mud, potholed as though it had been heavily shelled, and D.-D. said to Kerans as they lurched along in the jeep:

'If any wounded have to come over this road in those trucks, I shall be sorry for the poor chaps.'

Twenty-three miles over this going took them two and a quarter hours. It was 6.20 pm when at last they arrived at the headquarters of the 177th Regiment (or 'Brigade' in our parlance). It was at a small village about two miles beyond Ta Chiang called Hsiao Ta Chiang,[8] an assemblage of mud huts at the foot of the hills, smelling strongly of the farmyard. In the headquarters itself the regimental staff was ready for them and a plan prepared. To reach the *Amethyst* in her reported position off the island of Tai Ping, they were told, they would have to cross the Hsiao Ho at a ferrypoint guarded by Nationalist troops, but the trucks for the wounded would not be able to go any farther, for the crude road ended at Hsiao Ta Chiang; even the jeep and car could go only another short distance by a track. After that Shanks's pony was the only way. The regiment would therefore provide them with a party of stretcher-bearers and an escort of six soldiers, and the wounded would be carried back from the creek by stretcher to Hsiao Ta Chiang. This would be the assembly point for all wounded and from there they would be forwarded by truck to Chinkiang.

At this village they met also the Chinese correspondent of Reuter's. He showed them the message that Monaghan had given him of the desperate need for medical help, a message that served as a spur to them all. Kerans gave him another message for Nanking (which never arrived there) reporting on the progress of the party. They stayed here, however, no longer than they could help, for Kerans was itching to press on. It would soon be dark. So, leaving Packard's Pharmacist's Mate at the regimental headquarters, the rescue party set off again on what they hoped was the last stage of their journey. The jeep and the big American car lurched forward for a short distance, when the track petered out altogether and they disembarked.

---

[8] Approximate pronunciation: 'Shiaow da Giang'.

'Well, this,' said D.-D. with a smile, 'is where the navies have got to march.'

'All right, pongo,' retorted Kerans, 'you show us how. But we've got to push on; there's no time to lose.'

By the map, at all events, it should have been easy enough. Not four miles. They waited for the escort to catch them up and show the way, but there was no sign of the stretcher-bearers. Assured by the escort that the bearers were familiar with the way, they hurried on, but in case something had gone wrong D.-D. and Meh, as a precaution, hired two villagers for a stretcher and two others for a wheelbarrow, propelled fore-and-aft Chinese-wise, to carry the medical stores.

Thus re-grouped, this strangely assorted party of fifteen plodded forward as the sun went down behind them, casting their shadows longer and longer, not saying much in their urgency to get ahead, and moving in single file along a tortuous, snake-like path that skirted the foot of the hill called Ta Hung Shan, 814 feet high, crowned with its old pagoda. Meh and D.-D. cheerfully led the way behind a guide, while Kerans and Packard trudged towards the rear, keenly regretting that this was not their element. To men so pressed, the going was abominable, wandering deliriously among the paddy fields at the foot of the hill. Thus the three or four miles on the map became trebled, the sun sank behind the distant hills to their rear, the flights of duck flew home overhead, the mosquitoes thronged, the frogs set up their harsh night chorus and before long it was quite dark, the path a faint white serpent coiling over the ground and across the deeper dark of the innumerable ditches. The owl came out from his woody nest and the bats circled like swallows of the night. They grew concerned. Was their escort taking them to the right place? 'Yes,' they answered, 'this is quite right for the ferrypoint on the creek. We know it well. Not far now.'

Not until 9.30 pm did they at last reach the west bank of the Hsiao Ho, and, proceeding along it, come to the ferry-point. Looking about them in the dark, they saw the shapes of several junks in the water, a military watchtower and a group of mud cottages. Nothing else. All was silent with the dead quiet of a frontline position and not a soul was to be seen, until at length they came upon a boatman and his wife at the door of their hut. They asked him to take them across the creek, which was a good quarter mile wide here.

'It is very urgent,' they said. 'We *must* get across.'

'Quite impossible,' replied the boatman.

'Why? The Communists are not there yet, are they?'

'Oh, no: but the troops the other side have been changed today and we do not know the password. We should certainly be shot if we tried to cross tonight.'

Angry and frustrated, the four officers went into the boatman's hut to discuss what was to be done, in an atmosphere drenched with stale and unspeakable odours. Not till then did they realise how hungry they were. The British officers, expecting only a short expedition to Chinkiang, had brought no food with them, but the American said:

'Wait a minute, I've got something here. Don't know what it is. I just grabbed the first things I saw.'

He rummaged in his pack, produced some tins and, peering hopefully at the labels in the dim light, said:

'Let's see what we've got. Cheese. Sorry no biscuits, but it'll do. What's this? Well, well, of all things — Christmas pudding!'

They opened and ate hurriedly from the tins, and the boatman's wife then produced some of the thin, pale Chinese tea and little cups. 'I shouldn't drink from those if I were you,' said Packard, so, while the boatman's wife stared at such strange, foreign prejudices, they drank the concoction from the empty tins, enriched with the flavours of cheese and Christmas pudding.

Kerans was by now very worried and exasperated. The *Amethyst* might already have moved away, or would surely do so soon. Somehow they must get across that creek.

'We *must* get on,' he said. 'I've got to cross that creek somehow. Couldn't we telephone the regimental headquarters?'

'There would be no telephone here, I'm afraid,' Meh said. 'But there was a military post — a company or something — at the last village we passed through. They should have a phone. I'll go back there if you like and try.'

The further delay was serious, but they had to accept it. Accordingly, D.-D. and Meh went out and walked back to the last village and this time were fortunate. Meh struggled through to the regimental headquarters on the temperamental field telephone and, when he had put down the instrument, said to D.-D.:

'I was afraid so. We have come to the wrong place. We should have gone to a spot called Wu Chia Chiao, nearer to the mouth of the creek. It seems that the escort did not exactly know what our destination was. But the stretcher-bearers have gone to the right place and are there now. They are taking off the wounded already.'

'We shall have to hurry. How far is it?'

'Only a mile or two; but you know what these paddy fields are.'

Sending one of the escort back to collect Kerans and Packard, they hurried on again, making north-west roughly parallel with the creek, moving in almost complete silence and pressing on as fast as the serpentine track allowed. Only the barking of dogs as they passed through the sleeping villages and the raucous monotone of the croaking frogs broke the stillness. The night was overcast and dark; the white path, corkscrewing among the paddy fields, with stone slabs crossing frequent ditches, was faintly discernible but exasperating in its apparently lunatic course. Exasperating also was the enforced stoppage when the hired bearer sat down and refused to go another step.

At ten minutes to midnight, after they had been walking in all for five and a half hours, their steps beginning to stumble, they heard, breaking the brassy undertone of the incessant frogs, the sharper note of men's voices ahead. Hurrying forward, they ran into a party of Chinese soldiers, and in the murmur of voices heard an Englishman's. Kerans called out:

'Are you a British sailor?'

A form detached itself from the crowd.

'Yes, sir. Able Seaman Calcott. HMS *Amethyst*.'

'Thank God for that. I am Lieutenant-Commander Kerans, from the British Embassy. Tell me what the situation is.'

Calcott, who had been sent ashore from the ship in charge of the wounded whom Dr Chu Wei was evacuating, was naturally astonished at this sudden appearance of a British officer at midnight in a strange land. But, very collected and with the situation well in hand, he gave Kerans a clear picture of the position on board and ashore. Kerans now learnt for the first time that the frigate had moved to her second anchorage, in the mouth of the creek, not far from where they now stood, and was relieved to hear that she was still there. He was told that Weston was in very poor shape and realised that the casualties and damage were much more serious than had been appreciated. He learnt also that sixteen wounded had so far been landed, that twelve of these, including Skinner, had already been carried away by the stretcher-bearers, and that the other four, landed later, were at that moment lying at the side of the path ready to go. Kerans went over to them, bent down and spoke to each. The little Dr Chu, sterling fellow that he was, was still there, faithful to his humane task, wrapped in a blanket against the cold that had now invaded the night. A further batch of four severely wounded was due for evacuation, but of these Calcott had no information. Presumably they were still on board ship, though the evacuation had stopped and the sampan men had gone to their huts.

All this Kerans learnt from Calcott, and shortly after midnight a conference was held at the side of the path, for it was not at all clear what should be done now. In the event, it was decided that Packard and Meh should accompany the four wounded back to Hsiao Ta Chiang at once, so that the American could take charge of all the wounded at the assembly-point, while Kerans, D.-D., Calcott and Chu should try to get out to the *Amethyst* to bring off the remainder of the wounded and to deliver the Embassy medical chest.

Packard's party moved off on their long trudge at 12.30 in the morning of Friday, the 22nd, while Chu went to rouse the grumbling sampan man from his hut. The old man, unwilling to turn out again, was an unconscionable time doing so. Kerans and D.-D., shivering on the bank, fretted at the delay. They could now actually see the *Amethyst* in the distance, her slender, black bulk faintly silhouetted against the grey of the water. At last the old man was ready and the party hurried down to the sampan, which was in a small side creek bristling with reeds, loaded their medical stores and pushed off. It was providential, thought Dewar-Durie, that the boatman back at the ferry had been too scared to take them over the creek, for they had no knowledge that the ship had moved again, and, had they crossed, they would never have found the wounded.

Tired and cold though he was, Kerans felt cheered and relieved. The end of his mission was in sight. Throughout the long walk he had been plagued by the fear of being too late and had been urging the party forward. 'Reach her before dark,' Donaldson had said. Well, it was now just one o'clock in the morning but they would be in time after all.

It was a grey night, the colour of storm clouds. They could see the shape of their sampan outlined darkly against the water as the old man worked his sweep in the stern and they could hear the soft whisper of the wavelets under their bows as they moved. Save for these small sounds, a thick silence wrapped them in. No light was visible, no shape except their own and that of the distant frigate. A few minutes now.

Then Kerans exclaimed:

'By God! Look! She's under way. Can you see? We're too late.'

They looked, amazed, and their hearts fell. Maybe a hundred yards away, outlined against the background of grey waters, the slim, black silhouette of *Amethyst* was changing its angle of inclination as it moved a little to port. Then, with a trail of smoke from the funnel and a faint stern wave, she moved slowly across their bows, gliding silently upstream.

Impossible to reach her now. As a last urgent resort, Kerans got out his torch and tried to attract her attention by flashing her in Morse, but she gave no answer, floating like a ghost away into the further darkness.

They told the old man to stop, and for a moment the sampan lay idle in the dark and empty waters.

'It was,' says Dewar-Durie, 'very eerie. Not only were we terribly disappointed, but also we felt very lonely and helpless out there in the utter silence between two hostile armies. The sense of trespassing in someone else's war came home to us, and we were not at all sure that we should not be shot up by the sentries on our way back.'

Turning about, they made sadly and cautiously back to the creek.

CHAPTER 6: COMBINED OPERATION

AFTER RETURNING to the little creek the Chinese doctor took the British party, cold and disconsolate, into what appeared to be the headquarters of his battalion — the 2nd. It was a superior farmhouse enclosed within high walls. Inside, rows of soldiers were sleeping in double bunks around the walls, and in this fetid atmosphere, heavy with the odour of many bodies, Kerans, Dewar-Durie and Calcott rested for about ten minutes while an orderly made them some tea in the dim light. They were tired and inevitably felt a little bitter at having so narrowly missed the completion of their objective; for, though the main body of the wounded had been found and started on their way, Kerans was worried about the wounded still unaccounted for, and at having failed to take the ship the medical stores she so much needed. Two minutes earlier! They had been the victims of those small, incalculable mischances that so often frustrate expeditions. But there was plenty still to be done — the wounded to be got away to some place of safety and perhaps another attempt made to contact the ship.

After their brief rest, therefore, they got up to go. D.-D., producing his Embassy money, paid off the boatman liberally and offered some to Chu for his orderlies, who had worked so hard and willingly, but it was with difficulty that they persuaded him to accept anything. Then, at 1.30 am, Kerans, D.-D. and Calcott, together with a guide and with bearers provided by the battalion to carry the Embassy medicine chest, started on the long night walk back to the regimental HQ.

They took a different route this time — the right route, by which the stretcher-bearers had come and returned. Instead of running away to the south of the big Ta Hung hill, it went to the north of it by a col or saddle. The path, a rough hill track, quickly rose up the slope from the river bank, with stone slabs crossing the water courses among the terraced rice fields on the lower slopes. It was a very isolated and desolate part of the Yangtse, and the precariousness of their situation, trespassing in the front line of someone else's war, came home acutely to Kerans at least. They were all now pretty tired and cold, and Calcott, wearing only gym shoes on the stony track and feeling the strain of the last two days in the ship without rest, was soon footsore and limping. D.-D., however, whistled cheerfully all the way and kept their spirits up and what to the others was an arduous 'mountain' way was to the highlander 'gratifyingly shorter'.

Two and a quarter hours' slogging brought them back at last to Hsiao Ta Chiang at 3.45 in the morning, and here a ghostly sight met their eyes. Wrapped in ship's blankets, the dark shapes of the wounded lay silent at the roadside while Packard and his Pharmacist's Mate, with flickering torches, bent to give a transfusion of blood plasma to the Chinese pilot, and while the soft-footed soldiers, obedient to Meh's crisp orders, hurried out with water to the still forms who were crying out for it. The night crossing of the hills had been a torture for the stretcher-borne men, who had been very grievously shaken and were now very cold and spent. Kerans was saddened to find that the journey had proved to be too severe for two who had shown a special fortitude in their ordeal of nearly two days. Skinner, the Captain, and Ordinary Seaman George Winter of Blackpool, whose face had been blown away beyond all skill of plastic surgery, had both died in those foreign hills that cruel night.

Their bodies had been put to one side, away from the living. Kerans was further shocked to find that their watches and rings had been wrenched from them and their blankets stolen by the Chinese bearers. Close by, also put on one side as dead, lay two other figures. Kerans, passing close by, heard them crying faintly for water. One of them was Mirehouse. He was just alive, and the draught of water that was brought him perhaps saved his life. So serious was his case that, when at last they all mercifully reached safety, he had to be flown home for an immediate brain operation.

Calcott, who throughout the whole affair worked with unwearied devotion for his distressed shipmates, took Kerans round to each case in turn, to record their particulars and to say a word of encouragement. Kerans now, however, had a new problem. The two trucks provided by the Chinese Army headquarters were not enough, and a separate truck would be necessary for the two dead. He turned to Meh for further help, though well knowing the extremity in which the Nationalist forces themselves stood. Could the Army provide two more lorries? Once more Meh telephoned 4th Army and the answer came back at once from General Wang: yes, they would leave Chinkiang at once.

There was nothing more that Kerans and Dewar-Durie could do here. It was doctors' work. Kerans wanted, if it was still possible in the state of the war, to get all the wounded away to hospital in Shanghai by train. Accordingly, in the chill hours before first light, he and D.-D. drove off in their jeep to make arrangements at Chinkiang, leaving the doctor, who still had at least two hours' urgent work to do, to travel with all the wounded who could be got into the first two trucks; the remainder, and the two dead, would have to await the arrival of the two extra lorries promised. They reached Chinkiang at 7.15 am, pretty tired by now. Over the city there hung an air of sombre expectancy and great crowds were seeking means to get away. In a few hours' time a train for Shanghai was due in from Nanking and all well knew that it was likely to be the last. The two officers drove to the station. There was still one more thing they wanted and once again Admiral Kwei's word was to prove its worth. They went to the stationmaster and showed him the Admiral's letter. 'I want,' said Kerans, 'a first-class sleeping-car.'

'There are none here,' said the stationmaster, 'but I will try Nanking.'

He telephoned Nanking and when he had finished, said to Kerans: 'A sleeper will be hooked on at Nanking, sir.'

The first two trucks of wounded arrived in the city at about eight o'clock, and stopped first just inside the city gate at the American Goldsby King Memorial Hospital, one of those devoted institutions of mercy that sought to combine the work of healing the sick with the teaching of the Gospel to all who were willing to receive its word. This hospital was in the charge of Miss Charlotte Dunlap, who, having already been warned first by Nanking and then by Dewar-Durie, had already set up a ward with staff standing by before the arrangements for entraining had been made. On the arrival of the lorries Miss Dunlap, together with Miss Ruth Worth, the Medical Technician, and their Chinese nurses and male orderlies, came out, served the men with hot drinks and light food or administered morphia while they lay on their stretchers, and then accompanied them to the station. Here a seething crowd had gathered of all ages and sexes, making desperate endeavours to get away. Through this swarm, now swinging about and crowding thickly round them with that strange, detached curiosity of the Chinese, in which compassion has little place, the sailors were borne one by one from the lorries into the station, while police and porters struggled to clear a way. Miss Dunlap was still with them and she records a touching incident at this moment. 'I can still hear,' she says, 'a wounded boy saying to me on the station platform: "Nurse, will you fix my feet more comfortable?" When I turned up the Chinese quilt covering him, he had no feet.' This was Leading Seaman Cyril Williams.

Loading the stretchers through the windows of the train took a very long time. The train's departure was long overdue. Then, by what seemed to be almost a miracle, there suddenly turned up a lorry containing the four wounded who had been missing at the creek and whom Kerans had thought might still be in the ship. No one to this day seems to know for certain where and when they were landed nor how they came through to Chinkiang. But arrive they did, shepherded to safety by the care of the Nationalist 4th Army.

There was still no sign, however, of the lorry containing the bodies of Skinner and Winter. Kerans was desperately worried. Fruitless telephone calls were made everywhere. Reluctantly he agreed that the train must go, but as the stationmaster turned away, watch in hand, the lorry rolled into the station yard.

Packard was still giving an emergency blood transfusion on the open platform to one of the four wounded last to arrive. It was continued in the train, when the engine at last pulled out at twelve o'clock, by a Chinese nurse from the mission hospital who volunteered to accompany the party to Shanghai. She tended him throughout the journey and to her that man, whoever he may have been, owes his life. Packard and Calcott also accompanied the party.

On arrival at Shanghai next day, help came from every hand. The train was met by the Consul-General (Mr R. W. Urquhart), the Assistant Naval Attaché (Commander John Pringle), the Chairman of the British Chamber of Commerce, representatives of the United States Navy and a great crowd of other sympathisers. The wounded were taken first to the Country Hospital and then to the American Navy's hospital ship *Repose*, most generously placed at our disposal by Vice-Admiral Oscar C. Badger, and there they joined the wounded of *London*, *Consort* and *Black Swan*. For three days *Amethyst*'s men had lain on nothing but stretchers in the clothes in which they had been hit, receiving only emergency treatment and suffering all the distressing embarrassments of helpless men. On board *Repose*, however, they were rewarded with all the skilled care and comfort that the medical and nursing staff could give them till, a few days later, *Repose* delivered them to a British hospital in Hong Kong.

Skinner, at the special request of his wife, was buried at sea, as he would himself have wished, from HMS *Consort*. Winter, together with dead of the other ships, was buried in Hungjao Cemetery, with all traditional ceremony and with guards of honour provided by the British and American navies.

The whole episode of this 'night march' and the rescue of the wounded had been a splendid example of willing team work among mixed nationalities, of drive, pertinacity and fortitude. It could, of course, never have been accomplished without the unselfish and unstinted help of the Nationalist navy, army and railway staff, to whom no pains were too great. The railway, in spite of every effort by Dewar-Durie to pay for the coach, would accept none. The cause of humanity had been well served, and after this passage of years we may remember with gratitude what the forces and services of the Kuomintang did that night for our countrymen.

Meanwhile *Amethyst* was still creeping slowly up the Yangtse. When she had left the mouth of the Hsiao Ho, just after one o'clock that morning of the 22nd, having missed contact with Kerans so narrowly, Weston had insisted on going up to the bridge himself, fortified for the effort by a dose of benzedrine administered by Fearnley, who went up to the bridge with him to be at his side for further aid. Weston's movements were governed by a signal that he had received from FO2, which said:

> After landing wounded tonight you should have a shot at proceeding up-river before moonrise, which is about 3 am... You should proceed about 10 miles and then anchor. Only known enemy battery is about three miles up-river from your present position and after this you should be safe.

Navigating entirely by eye, Weston accordingly took the ship up-stream at about six knots, and at about 2.30 am, after some eight miles, he stopped to anchor before the moon rose. As the anchor was being let go, however, machine-gun bullets whistled about the ship again, this time from the south bank. Weston ordered the Union Jack on the port side to be illuminated, but this served to intensify fire rather than abate it. Surprised, and supposing that the Communists might already have crossed at this point, and not knowing what might be lying in wait farther up, Weston turned back for a mile and anchored safely at three o'clock, when, perhaps under the combined effects of the drugs and the strain, he collapsed.

While *Amethyst* lay there that fine, sunny morning the RAF in Shanghai were planning another attempt to come to her aid at the Navy's request. This time there would be no reliance on a boat or sampan when the Sunderland reached the river; she would have her own rubber dinghy ready inflated and would drop it the moment she came to rest, for a quick getaway would have to be made. She was to take back Monaghan, who had made a report to Admiral Madden in person in Shanghai, and she would bring also several relief officers and key ratings who had eagerly volunteered, together with a Naval chaplain to bury the dead.

Informed of the ship's new position, the Sunderland took off, again piloted by Letford, and just before 2 pm sighted the slim shape of the *Amethyst* at anchor in the sun. She tried to signal the ship by lamp, but the signals could not be read, and accordingly, after circling for about fifteen minutes, she came in to alight. As she touched the water and began to taxi, the dinghy was inflated, a door opened and Monaghan stood in the opening, clearly visible from the ship, ready to jump out the moment the aircraft came to rest.

But those fifteen minutes in the air had been more than enough for the Communist gunners to load and lay their pieces. They were already, no doubt, laid on the ship herself, and the flying-boat was certain to anchor close to her. The aircraft had barely come to rest on the port side of the ship and just astern when an accurate salvo plunged into the water close to it. The dinghy was launched while there was still some way on the aircraft, but before Monaghan or anyone else could jump in, it had broken loose, and Letford, with no option now, and with his wireless aerial shot away, opened his throttle and roared away again, remaining hopefully in the vicinity some forty-five minutes before returning to Shanghai.

For *Amethyst* it was just another disappointment. But as the Communists continued to shoot at the ship, Weston weighed once more. Up-river was as good a guess as down, so, while the Sunderland watched overhead, he proceeded on course, and the shelling stopped as soon as he was under way. Incomprehensible people. About three miles up, at 2.30 in the afternoon, he anchored again. Though now a very sick man, with his breath coming hard, and able to say only a few words at a time, he had taken the ship to her furthest anchorage.

Having done what he could for the wounded and the dead, Kerans went back to Chinese naval headquarters in Chin-kiang to report by telephone to Donaldson in Nanking. He had already learnt from Meh in confidence that the communists had made a crossing westward of Kiang Yin and that the Nationalists were going to evacuate Chinkiang that night. It was obvious that the situation was rapidly deteriorating and that the 'Thirty-sixth Alternative' was to be put into operation; there was no sign of any panic, but beneath the radiance of the April sun there was clearly a strained atmosphere in the air, like the hours and minutes of waiting before any great event. Whatever remained to be done must be done quickly.

From Kerans Donaldson learnt the serious situation on board the frigate. Donaldson accordingly ordered him to get on board *Amethyst* at all costs by any means that he could, have the First Lieutenant sent ashore to hospital and try to take the ship on up to Nanking. D.-D. was to remain at Chinkiang in case of further difficulties, to watch events and to see Weston safely off to Nanking.

To get to the *Amethyst* now seemed to Kerans an almost impossible task. Not only had the Chinese navy already refused him a craft, but also he did not know where the ship now was. Once more he turned to the Chinese navy, and once more, though with some reluctance, they answered his call, for the last time. No one could be found willing to take him but the young sub-lieutenant of the assault craft, who seemed game for anything. Just after two o'clock of that bright afternoon, little dreaming of the astonishing circumstances in which he would so soon return, Kerans said goodbye to D.-D. and quitted Chinkiang in this craft, taking with him again his precious load of stores, and taking also a set of Chinese Admiralty charts of the Yangtse, which were to play a vital part in that summer's drama. He passed through the narrow, fast and dangerous channel south of Silver Island, having no time to admire, as he had before, the island's romantic beauty, with its many temples sprinkling the dense woods that climbed to the pagoda at its peak. What he did see was Letford's Sunderland circling about, and he wondered what the sight might portend, for, of course, he knew nothing of the aircraft's second attempt to get to the ship.

An hour later, after hugging the south bank, unmolested by the enemy, he sighted, in the clear April sun, the objective he had been after for so long. He could observe no sign of life on her. Her decks appeared deserted. In fact, however, he came within an ace of being fired on, for Weston, not knowing now who was friend or foe, had given orders that any craft approaching the frigate should be covered by the Oerlikons. The Chinese sub-lieutenant, through his binoculars, saw this just in time, and Kerans ran to the bows of the craft and stood up waving his open charts flagwise.

On board, word of his coming had only just been received. As the Chinese craft came alongside on the port side aft, Kerans was greeted and helped on board by Walker. Having returned his greeting, Kerans said to him:

'That craft is to stay there. See that it does.'

Hett then came hurrying up and said: 'Glad to see you, sir. We have just heard about you. We are all in the W/T office.'

They entered the wireless office, and there Kerans saw Fearnley and Weston, who was seated. Having exchanged greetings and having overcome his surprise at seeing the RAF doctor, Kerans said to Weston:

'How are you feeling?'

'Oh, I'm really quite all right, sir; only need a few days' rest.'

'Well, you don't look it. What is your opinion, doctor?'

Fearnley was quite emphatic. 'He should be got to hospital as soon as possible, sir. His life may be in danger if he stays. I can't do anything for him here.'

'I'm afraid, then,' said Kerans to Weston, 'that you'll have to go. There is a landing-craft alongside. You must go at once, as the railway is likely to be cut at any moment. You'll find the Military Attaché waiting for you at Chin-kiang.'

It was the right and inevitable decision. Day, the First Lieutenant's servant, was called and he packed a few things hastily in a small attaché case. With this small provision, Weston was helped over the side and said goodbye to the ship he had served so splendidly and to whose company he had given so remarkable an example of courage and devotion to duty. He never obeyed an order more reluctantly and, to the last, spoke of 'coming back soon', as though he were merely leaving the football field to change his shorts.

Arriving at Chinkiang in the Chinese craft at five o'clock, Weston was taken to the naval headquarters, and Dewar — Durie, on being telephoned by Meh, came for him from the Goldsby King Hospital with Miss Dunlap in the jeep.

'He was sitting in a chair,' says D.-D., 'looking dreadful. Very white, his breath coming hard, and able to say only 'Yes' or 'No' in answer to my questions. We got him into the jeep and

I'm afraid that the jolting he got on the rough roads did him no good at all. We took him to the station, where Miss Dunlap gave him a shot of morphia.'

True to the end in his mission of friendship, Meh came with them to help with the railway authorities. The plan was to put the First Lieutenant on the next train to Nanking — the last one to go before the arrival of the Communists — where he would be taken care of by the Embassy. The train, due to leave at 5.30, did not go till eight o'clock, and, with the stationmaster's help, a seat was secured. All the time Weston, through spasms of pain, just able to walk, spoke scarcely a word. There was no one who could travel with him, for Dewar-Durie, as we have seen, had to stay in case he should be further needed to help the *Amethyst*, and he in fact stayed until the Communists were actually in the town; so Meh asked the Chinese sitting opposite Weston, who happened to be a member of the railway staff, to look after him.

It was a very bad journey for the First Lieutenant. He was very ill indeed. At some time during the night, very cold and empty, he fell into an uneasy sleep. When he awoke the train was stationary and the carriage empty. The Nationalists had blown up the main Nanking station and everyone had left the train. Major Geoffrey Cook, of the Embassy staff, had been sent to meet him. After searching for him all night, Cook at last discovered the train at Hu Ping station, was told it was empty and about to be destroyed. Not satisfied, he walked down the train and found a lonely man doubled up in a corner, unable to speak or move.

This by no means ended Weston's adventures, for he was determined to rejoin his ship by hook or by crook. After three weeks' treatment in Nanking University Hospital and a period of rest at the Embassy, he proposed to Donaldson that he should rejoin the *Amethyst*, where she then lay in captivity, by taking a sampan down-river. Donaldson would not allow him to take this risk and at the end of June got him away by train to Shanghai for a thorough medical overhaul. After only a week in Shanghai Weston made an effort to rejoin the ship that very nearly succeeded, the relation of which belongs to a later part of this story. Forced to go back to Shanghai by the Communists, he later on escaped to sea in a sampan disguised as a coolie, was arrested by a Nationalist warship on blockade duties whose captain did not believe his improbable story, but was finally, after some heated altercations, able to get transferred to a British ship at sea. Thereafter, because of the surge of Communist anger at the escape of the *Amethyst* and the fear of reprisals against those who had helped him to get out of Shanghai, he was kept strictly 'under cover', flown home to England in secrecy, and there at last rejoined his old ship after her triumphant return. He was shortly afterwards invalided out of the Navy, went to Cambridge, and is now a barrister.

CHAPTER 7: THE NET CLOSES

ALMOST SIMULTANEOUSLY with Kerans's arrival on board the *Amethyst* there came a signal from FO2 formally appointing him to command the ship. He had come with only what he stood up in, all his clothes and gear still in Nanking, and for the rest of the operation he had to live in borrowed clothes and with none of his personal possessions. Fearnley was in similar case.

Kerans's first task, and one that was much overdue, for the days were beginning to be hot, was to bury the seventeen dead that were still ranked on the deck and embarrassing the life of the ship. It was a bitter way to begin his new command and, as he says, 'I started my job with a nasty taste in my mouth.' Their preparation for this final rite had been put in hand on Weston's orders, ready for the expected arrival of the chaplain in the Sunderland, but had not been completed; and Kerans now ordered the final preparations of this disagreeable task to be carried out at once. They were then committed to the waters in twelve fathoms, each weighted with two 4-inch shells, Kerans himself reading the service for the Protestants, including one Chinese rating, and Petty Officer Stoker Mechanic Jeremiah Murphy performing the like office for the five Roman Catholics. For fear of Communist misunderstanding, no customary volleys of musketry marked their departure on their last passage, and their only salute as they passed over the side was the thin pipe of the bo'sun's call. Their names and memory are recorded in Part III.

This duty completed, Kerans turned to Frank and gave the order: 'Cox'n. clear lower deck. All hands aft.' The ship's company mustered accordingly on the quarterdeck, and when he appeared all hands looked up at him, silent and expectant, wondering what new turn in this strange story might now be in store. He told them first of all who he was, then gave them news of their wounded comrades and the deaths of Skinner and Winter, explained the general situation and told them briefly his intention. There was no change in *Amethyst*'s purpose. It was still her duty to reach Nanking and she would make the attempt that night.

This finished, Hett gave the order: 'Stand fast Chief and Petty Officers and Acting Cox'n. Remainder fall out.' To these senior ratings Kerans then had a more intimate talk. He wished first to get to know them all. He then gave them a more detailed review of the position, making it clear to them that it was a difficult and uncertain one. 'Do not,' he said, 'be over-optimistic. I know something of these Communist people and they are difficult to deal with. They are not normal by our standards. They will do their damnedest to get us down.' He then told them that, whatever turn events might take, it was his intention at all stages to keep the senior ratings 'in the picture' quite frankly, and it would be for them to pass it on to the rest of the ship's company in suitable form and terms. They were to be specially careful to check all false rumours and idle speculations.

Then he came to the most important matter. 'We may,' he said, 'have to face a difficult period, and I saw at once when I was speaking to the ship's company that we have a lot of very young ratings on board. So there will be a great responsibility on you senior ratings. A great deal is going to depend on your leadership and your ability to uphold morale throughout the ship. We shall need a spirit of complete confidence in ourselves and each other and I shall look to you to maintain it.'

His expectations were to be very handsomely fulfilled, for in the long days of endurance and trial still to come this little group of petty officers was to prove how decisive can be the influence of a fine lower-deck leadership.

Kerans then spoke to Frank about the special and pressing problem of Telegraphist French, who had been more or less continuously on duty for two and a half days without any sleep except for the few uneasy minutes that he could snatch between signals, with his head phones on, amid the incessant comings and goings and conversation of a room that had become the ship's command post. He seemed to have the submarine officer's acquired ability to rest without ever going to sleep, but obviously this could not continue and he was already having moments of light-headedness. Kerans therefore told the coxswain to discover whether there were any hands on board who knew the Morse code. As a result, there came forward Radio Electrical Mechanic Rutter[9] and Electrician Blomley, who had learnt Morse some years before but professed to remember little of it. However, they sufficed to give some rest to French by the simple plan of memorising the ship's call sign, SQT, which Hong Kong was asked to transmit at slow speed, and whenever it came over the air, if it was French's turn off watch, they woke him up. Later they acquired some proficiency themselves and were of valuable service. A restricted schedule of wireless watches was, of course, also arranged with FO2, and Madden was himself at all times extremely considerate, on more than one occasion personally ordering French to be stood off.

Kerans then turned to preparation for continuing the passage to Nanking, which he proposed to do that night. He reported his intention by signal to Vice-Admiral Madden, who was now

---

[9] He went down later in the loss of HMS *Affray*.

at the Saddle Islands at the approaches to the Yangtse in order to be close to events; but to his disappointment Madden replied that he was not to do so that night. For Madden had been advised by Stevenson that the passage could not be made without risk of further loss of life, the Communists having been reported (though incorrectly) to have crossed to the east of Nanking itself. It was clear that a rapid deterioration of the situation was to be expected and that the Taoist 'Thirty-sixth Alternative' had begun its course.

Amethyst's position became more and more uncertain. Away at the Saddles, Madden had been reluctantly considering the evacuation of her ship's company by Sunderland. His great anxiety, since we were not at war, was for the men. If the ship could not fulfil her purpose, or reach safety, he was prepared to lose her, distasteful though that was, if he could save her ship's company. What was unthinkable, however, was that one of His Majesty's ships should fall into the hands of the enemy. The logic of events pointed inexorably to the conclusion that the Communists intended either to sink or capture her. Rather than this, we should destroy her ourselves.

To the shocked surprise of the ship's company he accordingly made this signal:

> The safety of your ship's company being now the first consideration, you are now to prepare to evacuate from the ship and sink. Report when you will be ready.

When this signal began to come in Kerans was in the wireless office, and he stood behind French and watched over his shoulder as it came to its harsh conclusion. He was stupefied. The situation must have developed much more seriously than he had expected. It must surely be, he thought, the first time in naval history that an officer had been appointed to command a ship and then immediately ordered to scuttle her. Indeed, it must be the first time for many generations since a British ship had been abandoned without being reduced to extremity by battle or tempest. Besides all this, the sheer physical prospect was bleak enough; for everyone was tired out and 'to evacuate and sink' meant a swim of 500 yards followed by a march of 150 miles.

Preparations for obeying the order were put in hand at once, but Kerans asked permission to modify them in one respect. As there were no boats, and no sampans were available, and as many hands could not swim well enough, actual sinking in mid-river was not practicable. He therefore signalled Madden that he proposed to beach her instead, open all sea-cocks and destroy all he could, leaving ensigns flying.

These proposals received Madden's approval. He was a very human admiral, who in his mind and heart could perceive and feel all that was going on in that little ship far away, sorely vexed that he had been unable to reach her in her extremity, and looking all ways to help and sustain her.

> Ask me for any information you think I can give you [he signalled].

And then he added two memorable sentences:

> In a splendid performance by all on board the work of your sole telegraphist evokes my admiration. I cannot be too grateful for his help.

The night was already well advanced and on board *Amethyst* all preparations were made. The officers and senior ratings were summoned and Kerans, in accordance with his proclaimed intention, informed them of the order; to them as to him it was a tremendous shock, but they bustled to, and the individual leadership of the Petty Officers at once showed itself in the steadiness with which hands behaved. Destruction of all remaining radar equipment was completed, and methods worked out for destroying or setting fire to the ship. The ship's company were divided into three parties for the evacuation — Fearnley leading the first, Hett the second, and Strain the third. Kerans and the engine-room artificers would follow last after doing all the damage they could. Chocolate from Macnamara's canteen store and a small quantity of food were issued to all hands. The parties were to assemble on the shore and not move, unless forced, until the captain's arrival, when it was his intention to march by the banks of the Grand Canal to Soochow and thence to Shanghai.

All preparations for putting this plan into operation were complete by 9.45 pm, ready for the word. All hands felt the tenseness of the situation but remained steady and cheerful, though many were ready to drop with fatigue. More than ever the feeling grew that some great malignant cat was waiting for its helpless victim, and that from its clutches all ways of escape were being inexorably barred.

Half an hour later, while they waited, they saw the shapes of six small ships of the Chinese Navy proceeding downriver, fully darkened. They were, without doubt, ships that Kerans had seen in Nanking or in Chinkiang that day. They passed unmolested by the Communists. Kerans wondered if Meh and the smart young sub-lieutenant, who had been such good friends to *Amethyst*, were with them, and he wished them luck. A sense of loneliness began to descend on *Amethyst*. More of her friendly neighbours were going.

Just before midnight of the 22nd-23rd the tension was relieved when Madden, having meanwhile ascertained the views of the Admiralty and received some hope of diplomatic action, signalled that the order to evacuate would not be given that night. *Let your men*, he said, *have all the rest they can.*

The order was very gladly obeyed. Most of the ship's company were now able to get a few hours' sleep — virtually the first that they had had in three consecutive days of severe physical and emotional strain, continuously sustained. For Kerans, occupied with many problems, it was to be the second night on his legs, but it was better, he reflected, than tramping the mountains all night.

The next day, Saturday, April 23rd, dawned to a thick fog. It was St George's Day, a memorable date in the Royal Navy and the day of Zeebrugge, dedicated to the renown of that 'fiery mass of living valour, rolling on the foe', which had stormed ashore in 1918 against the German submarine stronghold. Would it for *Amethyst* be another memorable day, of a different sort? Was it to mark the unheroic end of one of the King's ships? Were her ship's company, who would have fought to the last round against their country's declared enemies, tamely to destroy a serviceable ship at a gunman's threat and to become refugees among a flying populace? For the enemies of *Amethyst* were now slowly closing in. During the night she had learned through Donaldson of a report from Dewar-Durie, still precariously standing by in Chinkiang, that all Nationalist troops and naval craft were now abandoning the city and that road, rail and water traffic would soon be cut off. All around the ship was a deathly silence and when the fog lifted at about nine o'clock not a movement was to be seen anywhere by land or water. The great river was deserted. On the south shore the friendly uniforms had gone. Even the fishermen hid anxiously in their huts. Northward the low thin line of Ta Sha was likewise silent and seemingly deserted.

Away at the Saddles on this anxious day, Madden was receiving such scanty information as there was about Communist movements, and he now put to Kerans a new proposal for saving the ship — that of withdrawal *down* the Yangtse.

> If I judge the prospect of making a down-stream passage reasonably promising [he signalled] would you feel it practicable navigationally at night?

Kerans replied at once in the affirmative, despite the lack of gyro and radar and a defective compass, but added that there must necessarily be a risk of grounding. The waters of the Yangtse were still low. No doubt Madden thought that risk too great a one, for the ship would then be in no better a position. A little later Kerans asked him whether, in view of the Nationalist withdrawal, he would consider it useful to move down the river a little at slow speed; to which Madden replied that he would prefer him to stay where he was for the time being, as he was sending out the Sunderland once again, this time on a mission of reconnaissance to discover what it could of Communist movements and artillery dispositions. *Amethyst* never saw the Sunderland, however, for, before reaching Kiang Yin Letford came under damaging machine-gun fire from the ground and had to return to Shanghai, his port fuel tank and other parts hit and the aircraft full of petrol fumes.

It was just after noon on that day of ominous silence that *Amethyst* caught her first glimpse of Communist troops. Away on the starboard beam Kerans observed the mustard uniforms moving about on Ta Sha Island and apparently constructing a battery to cover a crossing by their troops at this point. Kerans therefore concluded that his present anchorage would be too dangerous, and he decided to shift berth a short distance down-stream, selecting for his new anchorage a stretch of the river at the farther end of the island where there was no natural cover for hostile guns or snipers.

As he was about to anchor in the new position, however, accurate artillery fire was opened on the ship by a battery sited at either Yu Lung Chow or Pu Shun Wei. He immediately turned back at full speed and anchored out of sight of the battery a mile farther up, close to the south bank in twelve fathoms. It was *Amethyst*'s fifth anchorage since getting off the mud on Rose Island, and there she was to remain for a very long time, to endure an ordeal of a totally unexpected and distressful nature. Clearly the Communists did not intend that *Amethyst* should get either to Shanghai or to Nanking. The cat was waiting.

Except for this distant glimpse of the Communist troops and for this burst of hostile shooting, there was still no sign of life anywhere. The great, deserted river poured on its way to the sea, not a sampan on its surface. On the south bank, from the river's edge to the hills, save for the occasional whirring of the wild duck, not a thing was to be seen or heard. A great fear was upon everything. To *Amethyst*, alone in this great emptiness, the sense of desolation and helplessness was acute. The fear that Kerans felt was that, between batteries now both astern and ahead of him, he must expect to come under a withering cross-fire, to which, with only one gun and one Oerlikon, he could make no effective reply.

'The situation,' he said, 'now seemed desperate; there seemed no hope of movement either way, and a heavy loss of life was likely if any attempt was made. It appeared that the Communists could destroy us when they chose... Morale of all on board was still good in spite of the hopelessness of our plight. I realised, however, that it might snap at any moment and that breaking point had almost been reached.'

At one o'clock in the deathly silence of this St George's Day, however, they were able to pick up the BBC news which, no doubt on the strength of information given by the Foreign Office, said that a safe conduct for *Amethyst* was being contemplated. It was the first time that that magic word, so often and so hotly to be discussed in the next few months, was mentioned. The spirits of all on board were now low; it was a very bad period. But the BBC statement gave a ray of new hope, though of course no one knew how much basis there was for the statement. Kerans therefore made a signal to Madden seeking further information about a safe conduct and showing emphatically what his intentions were if attacked.

> Have just heard rough gist of BBC news. Is there any hope of safe conduct which I can pass on to ship's company, who are behaving splendidly but nearing breaking point. Have not been fired on again. If I come under fire before dark intend to beach, sink, destroy and reach Shanghai. Am ready to do this now.

An hour later came back Madden's reply:

> You have my approval to act as you think best if fired on again... I am trying to arrange safe conduct for you to Nanking but doubtful if this will operate quickly... Try to let me know if you have to abandon. I am full of admiration for all in *Amethyst*...

From signals that were passing between Madden and Donaldson in Nanking, everyone in *Amethyst* knew that Madden had appealed to our Ambassador to seek a safe conduct, but Sir Ralph Stevenson's predicament was that there was no central Communist authority with whom he could get in touch. Nanking was not yet in Communist hands (though it became so the next day), and the Communists' refusal to have anything to do with our diplomatic representatives at Tientsin and Peking did not encourage any hope of a new reasonableness at this stage. Our Consul in Peking had sent two communications to General Chu Teh in person by double registered post, but had so far received only postal delivery receipts for them. In this predicament, Mr Edward Youde, the Chinese-speaking Third Secretary of the Embassy, volunteered to undertake the hazardous mission of penetrating into the Communists' den with the intent of finding someone in high authority who would have power to give the ship a safe conduct. He crossed the Yangtse by ferry to Pukow, was conducted by the Nationalists to the front line of their bridgehead and, taking his life in his hands, walked alone into no-man's-land and into the fire that preceded the Communist attack. Having crossed it safely he delivered himself up to the Communist soldiery and was marched away, he knew not where, by cold, inhospitable faces.

All this, though in outline only, *Amethyst* knew from the signals that were passing. Youde, slight, fair and cheerful, was known to Kerans and a few others on board ship; he had served in the RNVR and was popular with everyone. The news of his dangerous mission on their behalf greatly heartened them all. They drank fresh courage also from a fine St George's Day broadcast by our Consul-General in Shanghai, Mr R. W. Urquhart. Then, in the afternoon, a new interest held the attention of all who were on deck, and they became spectators of an astonishing spectacle. The great stillness was suddenly broken. Ahead and astern of them the deserted river became alive with craft. From the creeks on either side of Ta Sha island on the north side two fleets sailed out, two motley fleets of all sorts of craft. They were Chu Teh's troops of the 'China People's Liberation Army' effecting their long-threatened crossing. For weeks these craft, the only kind of shipping the Communists possessed, had been creeping down the tortuous waters that led from the great Kao Yu lakes in the north. Here were no modern 'landing craft', but commandeered civilian craft of all sorts; junks, of which there were unlimited quantities of all sizes in the inland waterways of China, predominated; but there were also a few small motor craft, and even sampans were used in this great ragged Armada. A few well-served guns on the south bank could have sunk every one of them before they crossed the mile of water. Fortunately for them, however, it was no assault crossing that they now had to make, but a quiet, unopposed ferrying in a silent world. *Amethyst* watched, fascinated, but with no illusions that they were mere spectators at the ringside. They were very much within the ropes and the spectacle had for them too sinister a significance. Three miles astern of them they saw one fleet disgorge at the village of Tou Mien Shan, and ahead, little more than a mile away, the other fleet put ashore at Tan Ta Chen; Kerans smiled grimly when he saw that, as he had anticipated, his last anchorage lay precisely in the path of this fleet's crossing. Then the mustard-coats, with great quantities of infantry, mules and guns, spread out along the southern shore and presently were lost to view.

Night fell quickly and the ship was fully darkened, held alert as in the slips, awaiting what the night might bring. What it brought was totally unexpected, but fortunately *Amethyst* was now only a spectator. Out of the darkness upstream nine ships of the Chinese navy — destroyers, gunboats, landing craft and tugs — came steaming down. About 1000 yards astern of *Amethyst* one of them opened fire on Ta Sha island and in a moment there was a general engagement, both sides firing all they had. For an hour the noisy engagement went on, very wild and mis-directed, with shells landing all over the place and with no perceivable damage except for some fires on the north bank. The ships, thought Kerans, must have come from Nanking. The thought at once jumped to his mind that he should weigh anchor and follow in their wake, using them as pathfinders to the waters of freedom; but it came home to him that he was now not only captain of a ship but a political instrument as well — perhaps a pawn only, but one for the possession of which both white and black were to fight on the chequerboard of wits. If he identified himself with a Nationalist force, he realised, he would be in danger of imperilling a political issue. Moreover, he was only at half an hour's notice for steam, and they would be out of sight before he could catch them up. He set aside temptation, but a night was to come when a similar opportunity was to materialise out of the dark which he did not let slip.

It was the last opening of the gates of freedom, which now closed inexorably on either side of them. The enemy was all about, and no man could tell whether he would now pounce upon them. *Amethyst* was trapped. The retiarius had cast his net and the trident was poised. There now seemed no action that his entangled adversary could take. 'The isolation,' Kerans said, 'and the inability effectively to fight back, were acutely felt by all.'

PART TWO: 'A TURTLE IN A BOTTLE'

CHAPTER 8: THE COMMUNISTS ARRIVE

TO BE 'caught like a turtle in a bottle' is a traditional Chinese phrase that was only too painfully appropriate to the condition of the *Amethyst*. Let us meet the people who were responsible for this disreputable act and with whom we shall have so much to do.

We have seen them so far only in the distance, and have noted already that they wore a uniform of a strange mustard colour. Others have described it as ochre or 'dirty yellow'. As these yellow-coats come nearer, we can see that, apart from colour, they are dressed not very differently from the Nationalists. The uniform is of cotton, with puttees above naked ankles and thin-soled cotton shoes for the tough marching feet that can pad softly for fifty miles and fight a battle at the end. Slung from one shoulder is a loose bandolier in which the soldier keeps his rice, chop-sticks and his few toilet articles. For headgear he has a somewhat crude cap like an English cloth cap with the peak undone, adorned with a red star bearing a yellow symbol for August 1st. The flag under which he marches, singing organised propaganda songs, is red with a large yellow star. It is very noticeable that he wears no rank badges at all, so that it is impossible to tell a general from a private, except that an officer sometimes wears a belt.

Such was the appearance of the infantry of the China People's Liberation Army, or CPLA, whom Kerans and his companions were soon to meet. Inside the uniforms were men of peculiar mould. Great numbers of them had been fighting all their lives in one army or another, knew no other way of life, were physically as tough as the beasts of the field, and socially as crude and callous as humankind can be. Heavy drenchings of propaganda had leached away in them the cultured scepticism, the cool-minded defeatism and the 'Thirty-sixth Alternative' of their forefathers, and an aggressive positivism had taken their place.

On the other hand, the ramrod discipline under which they existed enforced certain soldierly virtues; extreme penalties were levied for looting, corruption and the maltreatment of civilians of 'liberated' territories. They took jealous care of their hard-won weapons, and the piece of red cloth in the muzzle of the rifle testified to the soldier's zeal in keeping it clean. Like all Communist armies, the soldiers of the CPLA were plagued with the fever of propaganda, injected at all hours by the political commissars, with one of whom we shall have a great deal to do. We shall see him at work in a different role, however, complete with his shorthand reporters and his ever-winking camera.

Fortunately for his peace of mind that Saturday night, Kerans had no inkling of what was in store for him. His one hope now was that Youde's mission to the Communists would succeed in securing for *Amethyst* a safe conduct either to Nanking or Shanghai. There seemed to be no earthly reason for refusing it. She had not the slightest intention of any hostile action against the People's Liberation Army; indeed, she was scarcely capable of it. All she wanted to do was to get away quietly without bothering anyone. Yet Youde's mission failed. He was led by devious and confused ways to what appeared to be a high military headquarters, though they would not tell him what it was. By those whom he saw he was given a cold reception and a flat refusal. The only terms on which they would, or might, consider giving freedom to their prey was that

Amethyst should assist the People's Liberation Army in getting across the Yangtse. This was a wonderful idea for propaganda, but was, of course, said Youde, quite unthinkable. 'In that case,' was the icy reply, 'you must find your own salvation.'

Amethyst learnt this by signals, of course, and was sorely disappointed, but she was getting used to disappointments. She mustered for church on Sunday morning, took steps by jettisoning top weight to correct a sudden list that developed, pumped out the flooded wardroom and repaired the leak with a cement box, reduced fire risks by jettisoning ready-use ammunition and fireworks, and went on with the tasks of repairing damage and getting the ship seaworthy as much as possible. During the day Madden signalled *You are much in my thoughts*, and a little later came a personal message of encouragement from the First Sea Lord at home. The larger significance of the Communist success, as they swept on unopposed far beyond the Yangtse, was beginning to be felt. British and American ships in the Whang Poo moved to anchorages out of range of Communist guns as they approached Shanghai. HMS *Jamaica*, 8000 tons, was ordered from Bermuda to augment the Far East Fleet. The United States announced that the cruiser *St Paul*, 13,000 tons, and the *Manchester*, 10,000 tons, would sail to China from Pearl Harbour.

In the centre of these troubles Kerans, in his own secret mind, without word or sign to anyone, began even from this moment to prepare for the possibility of enforced movement down-river as a last resort. He would not have been in the tradition of the Royal Navy otherwise. For the time being *Amethyst* was the pawn of the diplomats; but the moment might come, and come unexpectedly, when he would be told to fight his way out or even be obliged to do so by his own decision. When that moment might come, the circumstances, the reason, the justification, were all unknown imponderables; but he should be ready for it. To be so, the prime need was to make the injured ship as seaworthy as possible with the few materials that she had. Beyond that prime need there were many other factors on which he began to reflect as in his mind's eye he shaped the silhouette of things to come.

On Tuesday, April 26th, they had their first contact with the Communists, and very curious it was. All the morning *Amethyst* had been watching yet more of their army swarming across the river in great motley fleets, with the water very rough, when there came a hail from the shore. To Leading Steward But Sai-tin, who acted as Kerans's servant, having been sent for as interpreter, it was soon evident that the Communists wanted *Amethyst* to send a boat ashore. As the water was rough and the sole remaining whaler only partially watertight, Kerans declined. But when the demand was renewed two hours later and the river was calm, he decided to risk the whaler and called for a volunteer crew of strong swimmers, a call that was readily responded to. Kerans was resolved, however, not to risk any of his few officers, and he therefore, to everyone's amusement, took a lesson from the stage and dressed up Petty Officer Freeman, the Gunnery Instructor, in Strain's uniform. The purpose was, of course, to give Freeman 'face' when dealing with any Communist officer.

Freeman, who, as we have seen, was an intelligent and serious-minded petty officer, carried off his part extremely well. He was taken to a small, dirty farm in the neighbouring village, together with But Sai-tin, and, after having been kept waiting for an hour, was met by an officer who introduced himself as none other than the battery commander of San

Chiang Ying. He was a small man with a poker face and emotionless black eyes, and his rank and name, phonetically at least, were 'Major Kung'. Remember this. Freeman did not show himself in the least impressed and Kung then proceeded to make the astonishing charge that the responsibility for the episode was *Amethyst's*, as *she had opened fire first*. 'What!' exclaimed the astonished Freeman. 'That's quite untrue.' Kung then went on to say that, 'of course', he recognised that the frigate was British, and that he had given orders to his battery not to fire on British ships unless fired on first.

Kung then said that he was not empowered to give a safe conduct. That, he said, was a matter for higher authority in Nanking, but the ship would not be molested provided 'that there was no more trouble from her,' and that she did not move from her anchorage. If she moved, he would open fire.

Kung, however, was by no means hostile at this stage. Complaining of the damage done by the British ships, he disclosed that 252 casualties had been suffered by the Communist army, and Freeman now learnt that the Sin Ni Mu creek, immediately to the west of San Chiang Ying had been an assembly point for the CPLA craft, a fact that explained why this battery had been so alert and aggressive. As we may assume with some certainty, the bulk of the casualties and damage were in fact caused by *Consort*, not *Amethyst*, which fired only thirty rounds.

Kung wound up the discussion speciously by declaring that the 'British and the Chinese had always been friends.' At the end he even spoke English! This also we may remember for the future. Finally, before Freeman left, he inquired about future communication with the ship and, learning the state of her boats, said that he would arrange for a sampan to be at *Amethyst's* disposal in future; thus the ship would be unable to refuse to send a representative ashore when he wanted to see one.

When Kerans heard Freeman's report on this interview, he perceived very shrewdly that the truth behind all Kung's pretensions was that he had made a bad mistake, knew it, had been reprimanded by higher authority and was now trying to vindicate himself by false accusations. Little by little we shall see how the truth of it revealed itself only too abundantly. But if Kung was trying to vindicate himself to his superiors, the CPLA, highly sensitive to outside opinion, was equally anxious to vindicate itself to the world. Communism must never admit an error. The episode had to be treated, not on its merits, by factual inquiry and evidence, but as a matter for propaganda. Vituperative pronouncements by radio were scorching the air. Chinese territory, it was shouted abroad, had been wantonly invaded by foreign imperialists, who had made a murderous attack on the forces of liberation. Under provocation, the People's army had been forced to defend itself and had taught the reactionaries a sharp lesson. That was the Communist version.

The next day, after hands had mustered on the quarterdeck for photographs, of which Hett was the chief practitioner, a letter was delivered to *Amethyst* saying that Kung wished to see the captain. Kerans had no intention of leaving his ship at this stage in any circumstances, and he sent Hett, ever steady and devoted, in his place.

The interview was a perfectly friendly one, but again Kung's opening gambit was responsibility for opening fire. In vain Hett emphasised that *Amethyst* did not fire a shot until she had been hit several times and was driven aground. Nothing would persuade Kung to any admission. He was quite at sea about where *Consort* fitted into the incident and quite unaware that

Amethyst had already been fired on earlier on the 20th in the area of Yung An Chou. Kung went on to assure Hett, as he had done Freeman, of the safety of *Amethyst* and her ship's company, subtly recommending that she remained where she was. He also repeated that the grant of a safe conduct was a matter for Nanking.

Hett then presented Kung with a memorandum on three of *Amethyst*'s ratings who were missing from among those who had evacuated the ship at Rose Island and whose absence Heath had reported on arrival at Shanghai. This news had been signalled to Kerans the day before. One of the missing was Stoker Mechanic Maskell, of whom nothing more was ever heard and who was almost certainly lost in the evacuation either by drowning or from the Communist fire. The two others, whom we have already briefly mentioned and of whom we shall see a good deal more in this tortuous story of cat-and-mouse, were Stoker Mechanic Bannister and Boy Martin. They were believed to be in hospital at Wutsin, and Kerans now asked that they be returned to the ship if fit to travel. Kung said he knew nothing about this, but that he would forward the matter; and no doubt he already scented in these two young seamen a godsent and unexpected bargaining weapon. Finally, on Kerans's instructions, Hett asked for an interview with the CPLA general in Chinkiang, for it appeared obvious that they would have to go to someone higher than the battery commander.

When this interview was reported to Kerans, he was more than ever convinced of Kung's guilty conscience. It was inconceivable that he could genuinely have thought that *Amethyst* started the trouble. It was also perfectly clear that the shooting at *Amethyst* had been deliberate, not accidental. All the early hits she had received had been squarely on the beam, not glancing ones, which meant that the battery had waited until the ship was nicely in the centre of its arc of fire.

In the assessment that was finally made it was considered that the battery, in spite of Kung's denial, had in fact mistaken *Amethyst* for one of the Nationalist ships at Kiang Yin, which were believed to have given an undertaking to the Communists (as many of the Kuomintang forces did) that they would stay where they were and change sides after the crossing. *Amethyst* would therefore have been mistaken, by this particular battery, in spite of all her ensigns, as a KMT ship that was breaking its pledge. The whole basis of the Communist case, however, had to be that they must not admit an error, and it was therefore essential for them to pretend, first, that they knew the ship was British and, second, that the ship had fired the first shot.

These interviews Kerans reported in detail to Madden, together with his deductions from them. *I admire your comments*, replied Madden, and again a few days later:

> Thank you for your very interesting news. Good night. Your comments as usual are excellent.

For several days all was quiet. Civilian traffic returned to the river and, with continued heavy cross-river army traffic, *Amethyst* looked out on to a busy scene. Fleets of junks of all sizes came out again, breaking the low skyline with their fretted sails. A few motor craft and an occasional small steamship began to put in their appearances. To starboard of *Amethyst*, as she faced up-river, the low, thin line of Ta Sha island stretched out its monotonous length, unbroken by any eminence. To port lay the low hills. Straight ahead were the hills of Chinkiang, down which *Amethyst* could see the Communist convoys making their dusty way. There, too, lay the fir-clad cone of Silver Island, on which, wrote Ordinary Seaman

Mitchell, 'the first rays of the rising sun silhouette a pagoda which is reflected in the swiftly flowing Yangtse'. He listened to the orchestra of bird song on the south bank but felt 'a great hankering for beer and suitable blonde barmaids to go with it'.

In these last days of April, *Amethyst* was busy re-organising herself. She had lost over ninety hands and there was much to do. She mustered now only four officers, two of them non-executive, sixty-seven ratings and eight Chinese. Hett had automatically become Number One, Petty Officer White Chief Bo'sun's Mate and Frank, as we have seen, Coxswain. Macnamara, the civilian Naafi manager, was given the status and duties of a petty officer for watchkeeping purposes and won immediate approval by his natural leadership. Strain was appointed to take over general responsibility of the engine-room, and his ingenious improvisations in the shattered electrical services had an enchanted touch. Ordnance Artificer Rees, one of the outstanding hands throughout the operation, acted as 'schoolie' for the Boy ratings. Boy Grazier, of Leicester, donned the habit of ship's barber and before long did good business not only cutting hair but also trimming beards. A regular routine was instituted throughout the ship with a programme of training classes, of which the class in Damage Control was one of the most important. Fearnley prepared first-aid boxes for distribution to action stations and began a class in the subject; he found that hands took a keen interest in it and were mortified that they had been of so little help to their wounded shipmates when the doctor and SBA were killed. He was surprised at their lack of knowledge and even more surprised at their ignorance, as sailors, of artificial respiration. To correct it, he taught them the Shafer method.

Almost the worst off of all on board ship were the officers. Their wardroom, galley and all their cabins, together with their lavatories and baths (except the captain's), were destroyed or flooded, and soon became the resort of rats. Kerans therefore occupied the sea cabin, Hett the chart-house, and the other officers camp beds, coming up on deck when the weather turned hot, as it soon did. For the first week all the officers lived in the wireless office, eating out of tins. Later the holes in the captain's day cabin were sufficiently plugged to enable it to be used as a part-time wardroom as well as for its proper purpose. The officers, however, remained without their own galley and had the same meals as the ratings, brought from Griffiths's galley.

No one, however, was to have a more trying time than the engine-room department, and here Kerans soon found that he had a sterling and trusty hand in ERA Williams. Both the critical anxiety that was to arise over the ship's fuel and power, and the fierce, humid heat that had to be endured in the engine-room and boiler-room, were a severe strain on a staff that had been reduced by a half. They had lost six killed, six wounded and five evacuated. Yet, at the end of our story Strain was to report on 'the superb training of the engine-room ratings' and in due time the Fleet Engineer Officer at Hong Kong, Captain (E) F. V. Stopford, was to report that the engine-room department was 'fit for a Commander-in-Chief's inspection'.

There remained two other members of the ship's company. One of these was Simon, the ship's small black-and-white cat. He had suffered a few very small wounds, and a bad fright, in the shelling off Rose Island, and had gone to ground somewhere, but soon reappeared. He earned his keep by killing some rats, was a great favourite and had the run of the ship — except the captain's cabin, in which he unadvisedly abused his privilege.

Another general favourite was a dog called Peggy. She came from Hong Kong and was of the most suspicious pedigree. She was a pal of Griffiths's and certainly the galley was the place in which she was most interested. She took no interest at all in rats and her only other significant pastime, when hot weather rig was donned and nearly everyone wore sandals, was biting the captain's heels.

A diversion of a different sort was provided when the sampan that Kung had promised for their use duly arrived. It was manned by three women, and their arrival provided during the deadly months to come some slight diversion and occasional amusement. One was an old crone who was dubbed 'Granny' by the crew; another, carrying a baby, was 'Cheesi'; and the third was a young woman of passable looks whose name apparently was 'Midnight'; so, at least, she was called by *Amethyst*. They were, of course, the humblest kind of peasants or fisherfolk, but the sampan, which was their home, was kept spotlessly clean. They very soon became part of the ship's life, coming on board freely and wandering about the messdecks, exchanging good-humoured chaff with all and sundry. They were paid by a little rice and scraps of food and they welcomed even the 'gash' or refuse that was thrown over the ship's side. They were also delighted to have the unserviceable, oil-stained hammock which they were given and which they rigged as a sail. They showed a complete lack of interest in Communism and had no idea at all why the ship was there. *Amethyst* found this female 'side-party' a very willing crew, except in dirty weather, when they would not venture out. Like all Chinese boatmen, they seemed to have an uncanny sense when a storm was brewing, and if a typhoon were on the way the disappearance of sampans was a surer indication than official weather reports.

Before the end of April some very bad weather had already been experienced with high winds and rough water, for the Yangtse can change; and change suddenly, from a smooth, placid flow to an angry turbulence. On these days the river was deserted and *Amethyst* found herself more than ever alone.

May arrived, and Kerans could now do nothing but wait. On the afternoon of the 2nd, however, he experienced an agreeable surprise that filled everyone with new hope. A young Communist officer, who introduced himself as Captain Tai Kuo-liang, arrived on board by sampan and asked for an interview. Kerans, accompanied by Hett, saw him in his cabin, with But Sai-tin as interpreter. Tai, ignorant in such matters, came on board with an armed guard, one of whom accompanied him into Kerans's cabin. Kerans at once put him right on this unwitting breach of courtesy and Tai never again offended. In accordance with Communist practice, he refused sherry or other hospitality, but he was quite a pleasant young fellow, by no means, it seemed, an ardent Communist, but merely a willy-nilly follower. *Amethyst*'s officers were to see a good deal of him, and later on they were on tolerably good terms.

Tai was commander of a detachment which, it was soon seen, had been sent specially to keep watch on *Amethyst*. He now brought a message from General Liu Po-cheng in Nanking that agreement for a safe-passage of the ship might be given 'in a short time'. Tai could not elaborate further, except to add the usual remark that 'the General is very busy'. 'The most noticeable point about this meeting,' said Kerans afterwards, 'was that at no time did the question of who fired first ever arise. I felt that at long last we were really getting somewhere.' How mistaken he was to be proved!

It was all, no doubt, typical Communism. Hopes were aroused, and then for nearly three weeks there was a long tale of procrastination, excuses, false trails, and at the end a sudden change of front. Three times Hett went ashore to see Tai Kuo-liang and twice Tai came on board himself. Oh yes, he assured Hett the first time, he had sent a messenger to Nanking about the safe-passage, but the messenger had not yet returned; he would telephone again that evening. Two days later — an officer was due from Nanking with the safe conduct agreement in three days' time. And so on, repeatedly, with many variations. The safe conduct was always just round the corner. All this time there was no more mention of 'responsibility' for the incident or any nonsense of that sort. Nor, on the other hand, was the slightest information given, in spite of repeated requests, about the missing Bannister and Martin, although the Communists had long ago located them and, indeed, Tai's undisclosed superior had actually already removed them to Chinkiang and was keeping them there for his own twisted purposes.

Very soon the days of *Amethyst*'s captivity had amounted to a full four weeks without one single step having been taken to reach an accommodation. She was deliberately being fobbed off by a very junior officer who, though affable enough, was obviously nothing more than a watchdog and a postman for a principal who designedly kept himself unrevealed and out of reach until, having prepared his indictment, he was ready to declare himself. Kerans therefore, with Madden's approval, again made pressing efforts to get direct contact with General Yuan Chung-hsien, described as the Area Commander in Chinkiang; but here also Tai met him repeatedly with the same kind of evasive answer — he could not possibly approach General Yuan when he was 'so busy' on military matters.

Tai then began to take a keen interest in the eight Chinese hands on board ship, and said that General Yuan would like them all to come to a party (though he was 'too busy' to see Kerans on important business). Kerans naturally feared that this was an attempt to suborn or coerce his Chinese, most of whom had been showing unmistakable signs of nervousness. He therefore declined the dangerous invitation, but, when he was answered with a subtle threat, was obliged to give way. Off went the Chinese in due course, looking thoroughly miserable. However, it all proved to be very innocent and Sunday-schoolish, for all that took place was an inferior lunch and a temple service on Silver Island for *Amethyst*'s two Chinese dead.

Suspicion had fastened on But Sai-tin, who undoubtedly had the other Chinese hands under his control. He had become much too chummy with Tai and spoke wistfully of his native Wei Hai Wei in the north, though his family was safely in Hong Kong. However, he mended his ideas later, and by the end of *Amethyst*'s time in Yangtse was firmly convinced that Communism was the wrong horse to back. Kerans quite naturally never entirely trusted the Chinese hands; the safety and interest of the ship's company dictated that attitude, but in point of fact they were all loyal to the end.

Meanwhile much else was happening all around the ship. The harsh night chorus of the multitudinous frogs ashore could be plainly heard, and the cuckoo sang not only by day but all night also. The weather began to get hot and the ship's company changed into white summer rig, and in the afternoon and evening into unconventional dress, which gradually became less and less. With the heat there also came frequent stormy spells, the wind on one occasion almost a full gale with occasional very heavy gusts, and bad enough for Kerans to order steam to be raised. Except on these days, the river was extremely busy with both civilian and military traffic. Sightseers came and peered at the *Amethyst*. A small troopship sounded a bugle as she passed, a tug obscured its English name, and naval ranks on a motor launch, almost certainly deserters from the Kuomintang, hid themselves from shame. Nationalist landing craft converted to civilian use that had been captured intact at Chinkiang appeared on the river in increasing numbers. All these, and their habits, Kerans studied closely, storing the information in his mind. Kuomintang aircraft flew over occasionally on reconnaissance or small bombing raids, the Communists rattling ineffective machine gun fire at them from impossible ranges. Ashore, the south bank was busy with motor convoys or with military working parties singing their propaganda songs.

A working party of special significance was one that constructed a new battery on the south bank only half a mile ahead of *Amethyst*. This was very nicely sited, on a little cliff, to keep the frigate thoroughly well pinned down, but its routine task was an 'examination' or traffic control battery. Any craft not flying a red flag, other than junks was immediately fired on and brought in to the south bank for examination. Even those with red flags, however, were sometimes fired on, until a frantic sounding of sirens shamed the battery into silence. It became one of *Amethyst*'s amusements to watch the distant little yellow figures scuttling out to their guns every time a ship passed, obviously hoping for a chance to shoot. It was, however, a constant reminder of the gunners' alertness and of the promptness with which they seized on any opportunity of blazing off their pieces. The Chinese have always loved fireworks.

To avoid temptation to the gunners of this battery, *Amethyst* darkened ship every night on the port side. Otherwise on board ship life had long since returned to an ordered routine. The extreme shortage of hands kept all busy and there was weeks of repair work to be done. Every Sunday a church service was held and prayers offered for their wounded shipmates, as well as Sir Jacob Astley's famous prayer before Edgehill in 1642: 'O Lord, Thou knowest how busy I am this day. If I forget Thee, do not Thou forget me.' Everyone was in good health and down in the sick bay Fearnley and Howell had little to do. All hands were taking mepacrine daily against malaria (Paludrine being not yet available). The Admiralty, with great thoughtfulness, had been at great pains to keep all next-of-kin individually informed of the men's state, and individual telegrams to and from the ship passed freely by wireless telegraphy.

But there was a serious anxiety about food. Though there was ample tinned stuff, the supplies of fresh food had soon given out, for McCarthy, the Stores Petty Officer, whose business it was to victual the ship, had naturally expected to buy fresh supplies at Nanking. The ship held some small public funds in Hong Kong currency for this purpose, but these soon gave out. By the beginning of May the supply of potatoes was almost exhausted. Health demanded that fresh provisions should be obtained somehow, and Kerans, after a discussion with McCarthy, could see no way but barter. It was quite contrary to regulations, but there was no other way and Kerans obtained official permission.

Accordingly, through Tai Kuo-liang, arrangements were made for local contractors to visit the ship. They were two dirty little men, and with these creatures McCarthy began a long, wearying course of the most sordid huckstering.

Sometimes the haggling would go on for two hours, over how much sugar should be bartered for an egg or a pound of potatoes. McCarthy was at first staggered by the contractors' demands and methods, but he soon picked up the peculiar tactics of the game. The chief commodities with which he was allowed to trade were copper, duffle-coats, sea boots and a certain amount of flour and sugar, and with these he obtained sufficient eggs, bamboo-shoots, cabbage and potatoes to preserve a healthy diet in the hands of Petty Officer Cook (S) Griffiths, whose work, we may remind ourselves, in the words of the medical officer, was 'incomparably better' than the usual cooking in the Services. McCarthy, however, was not bargaining from strength, for he had to get fresh food at almost any price. The shifty-eyed contractors were not long in discerning this, and as time went on their rates of exchange grew ever more and more iniquitous.

So ends a relatively quiet phase in *Amethyst*'s story. Begun in strained anxiety, it gradually relaxed into an easier posture that called only for a little patience under the minor irritations of the inevitable Oriental procrastinations. No obstacle appeared in the return road to freedom and there was no need to consider any such dramatic steps as escape or self-destruction. The great thing now was to avoid provocation. The Communists were not such bad chaps after all.

Just at the end of this period Admiral Brind personally comes upon the scene. Arriving back in the Far East Station from England on April 30th, he had sailed up to the Saddle Islands in his dispatch vessel *Alert* on May 12th and presently took over from the sorely-tried Madden the burden of *Amethyst*'s problem. He was able to assure Madden that the Prime Minister fully endorsed all the hard decisions that he had had to make. Madden shortly afterwards sailed in *Belfast* for Hong Kong, where he continued to concern himself with the administrative or 'logistical' side of *Amethyst's* situation.

The close personal contacts that Brind had been able to have with the Foreign Secretary and the First Sea Lord were of great value in this peculiar situation and he was fortified by the knowledge that both Ernest Bevin and Lord Fraser would give him sturdy support. Both Admiralty and Foreign Office wisely left to him and to Stevenson generous room in which to manoeuvre on their own initiative. Brind's immediate instinct on his return was to proceed up the Yangtse himself, interview Yuan personally and bring *Amethyst* down-river under his own wing. Whitehall, however, did not approve of this proposal and, as events were to show, it is highly unlikely that the Communists would have allowed him to carry it out. Nevertheless, Brind continued to maintain a small force, though sometimes of only one ship, at the mouth of the Yangtse, to be ready to assist *Amethyst* as well as for any other emergency action — a measure that in time was to prove its value.

Thereafter, wherever his other duties might take him, even as far as Japan, Brind took personal control of the *Amethyst*, directing every move, polemic or tactical, within the boundaries of diplomatic policy, and doing his utmost to sustain and encourage the ship's company and their captain in the very severe trial that they would shortly have to undergo. Throughout our story, therefore, we must appreciate that *Amethyst* was acting under his orders, conveyed by wireless, though bedevilled by the lack of a secure code, and we must picture his tall figure as being present always in the background. He was, however, the first to appreciate that in such a situation a great deal may have to be left to the man on the spot. He therefore gave Kerans a wide discretion as to the manner in which his orders were to be put into effect and, by saying on occasions that 'you have my approval' to some course of action 'if you think fit', sustained him in the knowledge of the confidence of his Commander-in-Chief.

CHAPTER 9: THE COMMISSAR

THE STORY of the *Amethyst* now enters a new phase, one that we may legitimately call the most grim. In spite of the heat below decks, the anxieties about food, the lack of any mail for four weeks and the strain of a vexatious captivity, the ship was in good enough heart, expecting that the word for her release would shortly come; it was only a matter of a little patience in the face of Oriental delaying tactics. During the past weeks of waiting, the dropping of Kung's original charges of 'responsibility' and the nature of relations with Tai had led Kerans to suppose that no serious difficulties lay ahead, other than the usual procrastination.

That expectation, however, was now to be rudely shattered. During all these weeks the Communists had in fact taken no steps at all towards the provision of a safe conduct. What they had been doing, in that exhaustive, searching, intense manner of theirs, was preparing the 'front' that they were going to present over the whole business. The case had been painstakingly prejudiced and the accused would now be called upon to plead guilty. Thus it happened that late on the hot afternoon of May 18th two young Communist officers, who spoke English, came on board to see Kerans. There followed a long and frigid interview. They began by presenting Kerans with a written memorandum that took him completely aback. The memorandum was from what was described as 'Frontier Headquarters Chin-kiang Area' — the administrative formation that General Yuan Chung-hsien commanded. This headquarters, the memorandum said, had 'decided' to solve by negotiation the responsibility that ought to be assumed by HM ships which have done the brutal acts on 20 April in invading the battle front of the China People's Liberation Army.

For the purposes of these negotiations, the memorandum went on, General Yuan had appointed Colonel Kang Mao-chao, Political Commissar of the 3rd Artillery Regiment, as his representative. The British Commander-in-Chief was accordingly required to appoint Kerans or some other officer formally to represent him in like manner.

Astonished at this turn of events and at reversion of the arid question of 'responsibility', Kerans replied to the officers that this was a serious political issue that could not possibly be left to an officer of his rank, but was for the highest possible diplomatic levels in Nanking. To which the officers quickly retorted that as diplomatic relations had not been established by the Communists the matter would have to be settled locally — which was the opposite of what 'Major Kung' had said originally. But, they added acidly, it would not be discussed any further until a meeting had been convened, and that meeting itself could not take place until Kerans's credentials as the Commander-in-Chief's authorised representative had been accepted. Nor would the Communists consider the liberation of Bannister and Martin until that meeting. They closed the interview by observing pointedly, as all these Communists were so fond of doing, that any attempt by *Amethyst* to move would draw the fire of their batteries.

Here, then, was a new and much stiffer situation. The cat was going to scratch again. Another course of long and tedious prevarications under pressure seemed to lie ahead. Kerans reported in full to the Commander-in-Chief who, in turn, had to consult the Ambassador and the Admiralty.

Four days later, there came a long signal from the Commander-in-Chief instructing Kerans to convey a personal message from him to General Yuan, in which the procedure that ought to be followed for settling matters was logically outlined. As this exposition was to underlie the whole of the rest of the battle of wits, we shall set out (in our own terms) the main points of it here:

(a). Captains of frigates are not the proper persons to negotiate on international responsibilities. These are for high diplomatic levels, and discussions had, in fact, been started by the British Ambassador in Nanking with the Communists' Foreign National Affairs Department, Moreover, the present commanding officer of the *Amethyst* could not speak with direct knowledge of this incident, because he was not there.

(b) The question of safe conduct for the ship to return downriver, however, was a local one, governed by military conditions only, and capable of being settled without prejudice to the political issue of responsibility. No military grounds now exist for refusing a safe conduct, and detention of the ship on any other grounds would have serious international consequences.

(c). Lieutenant-Commander Kerans was authorised to represent the Commander-in-Chief in explaining any point that was not clear and to make arrangements for the safe-passage, though he could not be authorised to discuss international responsibilities.

These grounds the Commander-in-Chief, always in close consultation with the Admiralty and with the Ambassador, was to maintain consistently throughout the whole imbroglio.

Armed with these instructions, Kerans left the ship on May 24th in response to a summons to a meeting from Kang Mao-chao, the Political Commissar. As he stepped into the sampan, dressed carefully in the smartest uniform that could be found in the ship, his mind was heavy with doubt. He had no inkling of what might lie ahead, of what outrage might be committed or of what hornet's nest he might run into; but he was certain that the meeting would be a tough one. This sort of thing was emphatically not the business of a naval officer.

He was met on shore by Tai and, amid the curious stares of the peasants and the yellow-clad soldiery, escorted by him on a walk of about a mile and a half before they reached a road, where they were picked up in a captured American command car (from which, except for the tyres, all traces of American origin had been carefully removed) and driven over the vile, dusty road to Yuan's headquarters in Chin-kiang.

In this hostile world Kerans was quite alone, without an interpreter. He felt all eyes upon him as he re-entered Chin-kiang and beheld it under its new masters. The sun beat down on the narrow streets, dusty and crowded, and among their flaunting signs the peculiar odours of a Chinese city — the faint, sweet scent of herb shops, the heady aroma of food frying in deep fat with spices, the stale smell of human bodies and the pervading undertone of excreta — hung in the air and accentuated the rising heat. The yellow-clad soldiery and the dark-blue civilians padded noiselessly in the dust, tokens of an unhurried world.

But beneath all this was a new tautening — a tension and a grip. For Kerans the atmosphere was very critical. The fate of a ship, the lives of some eighty men and, above all, the good name of a great nation hung upon how he was to carry through a battle of polemics in which he had had no training. This was a politician's job, not a seaman's. He knew now that he would have to fight, not merely for the safe-passage of his ship, but for his country's honour. He would need all his wits about him, but there were certain things on which he was determined to stand firm at all costs.

In this frame of mind did this Daniel, slightly aloof and cynical, in borrowed uniform, step from the car, pass the sentries, traverse a courtyard, and enter the Communist lions' den. And what a den! Within a big, thick-walled, grey stone building all the panoply, the blare and the showmanship of propaganda flaunted their apparatus. Green garlands festooned the building and an enormous, 'blown-up' photograph of Mao Tse-tung's slab-like visage affronted the eye at the very entrance, and again inside; indeed, it was everywhere. Indoors the pencils of the Communist Press were itching to record a story of British humiliation and the camera hung ready to wink its eye. All was carefully staged. A long table in a large, bare room, with a stage at the end and a stove in the corner — very like a mess — stood ready for the performance.

In this setting, with another great photograph of Mao staring at him, Kerans met General Yuan. He was a short, round man, bland of face and by no means bearing the semblance of a hard-bitten warrior, well-educated and later to be Ambassador to India. Kerans handed him the Commander-in-Chief's personal message and they all sat down at the table, with the woman photographer's camera clicking away, taking shots of Kerans from all angles. She was a tall, flat-bosomed, apathetic, Amazonian creature. Yuan was supported by the political Commissar of whom Kerans had been told, Colonel Kang Mao-chao; and in him Kerans beheld a well-fleshed, bullet-headed man with black, close-cropped hair, of cold, hard visage, stiff and severe in manner. As it turned out later, Kang was a Peking lawyer. He was a bitter an. uncompromising Communist, and it was to be with this intractable opponent, this slab of concrete, that Kerans was to have to fight so long and devastating a battle of wits. It was he who was the real cat outside the mouse-hole. Besides these three, there were two weedy little reporters and two interpreters, one of whom was Captain Jen Hsin-wei, a fiery young Communist from Kunming University.

Facing this array, with all these hostile eyes fastened on him and the camera winking freely, Kerans felt very lonely; and he was to feel more lonely still before the meeting was over, for very quickly he found himself facing an opponent who was not interested in discussing facts, but had prepared an ultimatum based on a pre-arranged falsification of them. Everything was fabricated on the well-known thesis that 'Communism must never admit an error' and that the prisoner was required to plead guilty before evidence. The atmosphere was extremely tense and forbidding.

Yuan, having read Admiral Brind's letter, began the meeting by replying to it with the most extraordinary proposition. *Amethyst*, he said, had 'invaded' CPLA territory and had fired on their batteries. He could not consider the grant of a safe-passage, he now told the amazed Kerans, until the British Fleet first admitted their guilt. Details of the exact degree of responsibility and of the compensation to be paid could be left for negotiation subsequently, but there must first be an acknowledgment of blame by the British.

'I am not empowered to discuss that,' replied Kerans, astonished at this extraordinary attitude. 'An officer of my rank could obviously never be authorised to discuss a matter of such importance. That is a political matter, to be dealt with by our Embassy. My sole concern is to procure a safe conduct for my ship.'

'I observe,' said Yuan, 'that your admiral says that negotiations are proceeding in Nanking. That is not true. The

Foreign National Affairs Department has no such authority. The matter is to be decided here and I shall not discuss a safe conduct until you accept responsibility for this act of violence against the CPLA.' With that he got up and left the meeting. The chair was then taken by Kang. He opened his attack — for attack it was — by presenting to Kerans a memorandum for Admiral Brind of the most preposterous nature. It contained three main articles. The first reiterated that *Amethyst* and other warships had committed 'brutal' acts by 'invading' CPLA territory. The second declared that *Amethyst* 'purposely provoked and fired the first shot. Once again the British Fleet sent its warships to reinforce in attacking with gun-fire the battle-front of the CPLA'. The third article alleged that *Amethyst* and other warships 'coordinated' with Kuomintang forces and hampered military operations of the CPLA, thereby producing a situation 'advantageous to the Kuomintang'.

These 'facts', the memorandum went on, were widely known and 'could not be altered'. The British must take full responsibility and must fulfil the following demands:

(a). Acknowledge that such actions by the British warships were wrong and apologise for them to the CPLA, and

(b). Promise to pay compensation for the damage sustained by the CPLA and the people.

The fulfilment of these demands was a pre-requisite to any negotiations on a safe conduct.

Having listened to this startling document, and keeping his temper with difficulty, Kerans thought it best not to argue its points in too much detail at the present juncture, but to demonstrate that, in every aspect of the military and political situation, 'invasion' was a gross misuse of words. Then followed a grim, protracted and sterile argument. Towards the end of it Kerans felt some easing of the tension. Kang uttered some platitude about Sino-British friendship and Kerans, remembering the sensitivity of the Communists to world opinion, seized his opportunity.

'I quite agree,' he said. 'If you subject my ship's company to further hardship you will certainly damage Sino-British relations and you will damage your name in the world at large.'

'What are these hardships?' asked the Commissar sharply. 'The Chinese Army bears no ill-will to your men.'

'In the first place,' Kerans replied, 'you are still detaining two of my wounded men at Wutsin.'

'Very well, I will see that they are returned to you, provided you make a formal request in writing.'

'I have done so already, but I will do so again now. I have repeatedly asked for their return. We are also beginning to suffer on board ship because of the shortage of provisions and fuel. It is beginning to get hot, I am having to economise fuel, and conditions at night will soon be unpleasant.'

Kang replied that Keran's Chinese would have liberty to buy provisions for the ship, but he refused to recognise that the detention of the ship imposed any responsibility on the Communists to provide her with food and necessities. The prisoner must somehow fend for himself if he refused to submit. Why sustain the morale of men whom you intend to beat into submission? As to the fuel problem, which we shall come to in a moment, it was weeks before Kang realised that the ship did not burn coal!

The few examples that we have seen so far of the signals passing between Brind and Kerans show already how embarrassing to both was the lack of a 'secure' telegraphic code, due to the destruction of all secret books at Rose Island. The Commander-in-Chief could not speak freely to Kerans, nor discuss, as he wished to do when things got really bad, the possibility either of a breakout by *Amethyst* or of a break *in* by the Fleet, which he more than once contemplated. Indeed, we shall see the two officers at cross-purposes at one critical moment, through attempts at veiled suggestion. It was a major difficulty, bedevilling all transactions.

CHAPTER 10: THE HOSTAGES

IN THE matter of Bannister and Martin, Kang was true to his word. We shall see why. The appearance in our story of these two young sailors gives us an opportunity to fill in a gap that their absence has made, and for this purpose we must turn back the pages of the calendar for some five weeks in order to follow their curious fortune and that of their shipmates who landed on the shores of Rose Island on that anxious and confused day of April 20th.

We have heard the evacuation order on that date and we have seen hands go ashore, somewhat confusedly, some seventy or more of them. We have seen how Monaghan, Wilkinson, French and some others returned to their ship, but how the two parties into which the remainder had become divided were unfortunately taken over to the mainland and conducted by the Nationalists some miles away from the river, whence they were not allowed to return to the ship.

Several of those who went ashore had been wounded. Two of these were Stoker Mechanic Samuel Bannister, a fresh-complexioned young Northern Irishman of twenty-one from Belfast, and Boy Keith Martin, aged seventeen, a tall, thin, rather serious young fellow, though with a humorous face. Both were new to the ship, having joined at Hong Kong. Martin had been wounded in the buttock, and Bannister had been hit while below deck, a shell splinter lodging in his chest against the right branch of the windpipe. It was a very painful wound, making breathing difficult, and Alderton, shortly before he himself was killed, had given him a shot of morphia. Bannister was one of the four put into the whaler, which, as we have seen earlier, was nearly capsized by a shell burst. He found himself alone in the water and was all but drowned, but just managed to scramble to the beach, where hands came forward to pull him up the bank and into the concealment of the long grass and bamboo.

While the party under Monaghan and Ordnance Artificer Warwick were conducted to the island headquarters, Bannister and Martin found themselves with the party of which Chief Petty Officer Heath took charge. This party, many of them in nothing but their underclothes, made their cautious way on hands and knees to the cover of the south side of the island, Bannister crawling with great pain. A Chinese cook, having come ashore in the whaler immaculately dressed, declined to obey the order to take cover, despite the whine of the bullets, saying: 'Me no crawl; me got best suit.' At the south bank a Chinese messboy, with no little courage, swam across to the mainland, and the Nationalist troops there sent over some sampans and ferried the whole party across. The party, numbering about thirty, was led up to a group of evil-smelling huts, and here the soldiers brought Nationalist uniforms for those who were only in underwear, of whom Heath himself was one. No shoes were provided, however, and those who had none were compelled to go barefoot for the long march that lay ahead. Here also Petty Officer Telegraphist Mewse and Petty Officer Bowles went in search of a field telephone in order to report to Monaghan, but without success.

In the early afternoon, hurrying down at the sound of gun-fire to the front line on the river bank, they watched with emotion the whole of *Consort*'s action, British and Chinese joining in cheers at her spectacular bombardment and splendid handling. Immediately afterwards they were called together by a Chinese officer, and set out under guides upon a march inland. Bannister was now carried on a stretcher by four Chinese. The little column looked a queer and motley collection in their mixed clothing, and those without shoes were soon in distress. Late in the afternoon they stopped for a rest at a large village, a few miles inland, and were joined by the party of about twenty-five under Ordnance Artificer Warwick.

It was from here that Heath spoke to Monaghan on Rose Island by a Nationalist field telephone and that the unavoidable decision had to be made for the evacuated party to make for Shanghai. At about 6.30 pm, therefore, Heath and Warwick led out their party again, under Nationalist guides, for yet another weary march. Night fell, and at about 9.30 they came to a group of buildings somewhere on the Hsiao Ho where they mercifully stopped. The feet of those without shoes were bleeding, all were exhausted and hungry and here young Martin collapsed.

After about three hours' rest they were roused again, soon after midnight, and were led to a craft in the Hsiao Ho, but the two senior petty officers learnt to their dismay that Bannister and Martin could not go with them. They must rest for the night, said the Chinese medical orderly, or 'they finish'. Heath argued with him through an interpreter, but he only repeated firmly: 'They stay or they finish.' After promises that the two young hands would be sent on the next day, the main body crossed the creek, at about the same time as *Amethyst* was freeing herself from the mud, embussed in ex-American lorries and were driven to the large town of Wutsin (or Chang Chou). Here Heath telephoned the British Consulate in Shanghai and the party was bedded down for what was left of the night. The next day they were entrained for Shanghai, where they were drafted temporarily to HMS *London*, and disappear from our story.

But not Bannister and Martin. The boy and the young Belfast stoker-mechanic awoke on the morning of the 21st and were dismayed to find themselves separated from their shipmates. They had had a very bad night, but they were in kindly, though perhaps rather rough hands. Another long and weary stretcher journey lay ahead of them for a day and half a night, to be followed on April 22nd by a tormenting ride over vile roads, before they arrived at last at Wutsin. Here, shaken and exhausted, they were received into the shelter of the Christian mission hospital. It was three days since they had been hit and, except for the morphia that Alderton had administered to Bannister, they had not all this time received any trained medical attention.

The whole story of this evacuation of the Rose Island parties is another shining example of the lengths to which the Nationalists were prepared to go to succour our countrymen, for whom, though we were neutrals in this civil war, they entertained the feelings of ancient friends and allies in the recent war against Japan. The organisation of this evacuation at such a time must have been a severe tax on their strained communications and their staff, and the long and arduous march of the humble stretcher-bearers, cheerfully performed, was a service to which some of our men owe their lives.

At the hospital kindly Chinese hands attended to the two young British ratings. The Wutsin hospital seems to have been at this time staffed entirely by Chinese. Bannister was X-rayed and told that he would be operated on at once for the extraction of the shell-splinter bearing against his windpipe. He was put on to the operating table and the Chinese doctor, English-speaking, bent over him and said:

'I am sorry, but we no longer have any anaesthetics. I fear it will hurt.'

The young stoker was startled; he had not expected this. But he said quietly: 'Go ahead,' and bore his ordeal with fortitude.

Two days later, after a day of strange quiet and anxious expectancy, the Communists occupied the town.

The hospital, true to its mission, carried on, and the two British sailors stayed on for about another fortnight, their wounds healing. Then, somewhere about May 8th, they were sent for by the Communists and, wearing hospital dressing-gowns and wondering what their fate was to be, were put into a lorry and driven to Chinkiang.

Note this date. It had been on April 27th that Kerans had asked in writing for their return to the ship, and he had since made repeated inquiries for them. In Chinkiang the two men were well enough treated, though moved from one house to another, always, of course, under guard. They were given Chinese coolie clothes and adequate food, but hard beds. They appeared before Kang and were subjected to all his wiles, both by veiled threats and by cajolery, with all the skill and subtlety of the trained Communist inquisitor — though never with force or duress — to extract from them an admission that, on that notorious twentieth day of April, *Amethyst* had fired the first shot. To their everlasting credit they steadily and stubbornly refused, and clung to the truth. Nor did friendly chats upon the virtues of Communism by a smiling and jestful interpreter — probably Jen Hsin-wei — fall upon receptive soil.

All this, bear in mind, took place before Kang had had his first meeting with Kerans; by that date the two young sailors had already been in his charge for some sixteen days.

We can see here clearly revealed the cogs, gears and springs of Kang's mental machinery busily at work. Here are two raw lads, one a mere boy of seventeen, delivered into his hands —

two unexpected aces dealt him from the pack by Kerans himself. First, he will treat them reasonably well, allow their guards to get chummy, and will soften them for his grand objective, which is to extract a confession of *Amethyst*'s guilt; that will, he thinks, cut the ground from beneath Kerans's feet. Again, whether they 'confess' or not, they will be good merchandise to bargain with and, in that typical Communist tactic, he can generously hand them over to his opponent, in order to raise his hopes, fully intending to dash them at the next meeting with some stronger demand.

After his first meeting with Kerans on May 24th Kang decided that his hostages were of no more use to him. He had got no 'confession' from them. Now he would use his cat tactics. Accordingly, the very next day, the two young men, wearing their coolie suits, were brought down to the village nearest *Amethyst*'s anchorage by Tai and Jen, and handed over to Hett among scenes of planned *cameraderie*, with the peering photographer taking quick shots of sudden, unexpected hand-shakes.

The two youngsters naturally received a rousing and good-humoured welcome from their shipmates when they came on board. They had brought with them a letter to Kerans in which Kang said:

> These two ratings have been given medical care and have been provided with necessary supplies by the China People's Liberation Army. It is for the friendship between the people of China and the people of Great Britain that we have given them friendly treatment.
>
> Now it is also for the friendship of the people of China towards the people of Great Britain that we send them back to the ship.

The 'medical care', however, was not evident. None had been given by the CPLA; all had been done by the mission hospital. On arrival on board the two were sent at once for a medical inspection by Fearnley, who found that Bannister had contracted scabies from contact with his guards and that he had an untreated ulcer on his shoulder.

Another welcome arrival in the ship a few days later, by permission of the Communists, was a Chinese translator on Donaldson's staff at Nanking. He was generally known as Sam Leo, in similitude of his real name, which was Liu Chin-tseng. He had volunteered in response to Kerans's appeal for an interpreter more reliable and more educated than But Sai-tin, who was not up to the exacting standards of interpretation needed for the political battle of wits that had begun, in which, before long, the precise meaning of a single Chinese character was to have a critical significance. Middle-aged, fairly tall, spectacled, rather diffident and studious, Leo was a man of integrity of the old school. He was messed on board as a Chief Petty Officer and became very popular with the ship's company, for whom he did excellent service. Not only did he serve Kerans as an interpreter both orally and in documentation, but he also managed somehow or other to make an occasional journey to and from Nanking. He was never, of course, entrusted with anything that might compromise him when searched, but he was a useful link with the outside world, and was able to bring the ship badly needed money and penicillin from the Embassy and to do small shopping trips. *Amethyst*, obliged by harsh necessity at the end to leave him to the mercy of the Communists, has much cause to be grateful to his memory.

CHAPTER 11: KERANS *VERSUS* KANG

THE BATTLE between Kerans and Kang was now in full swing. It is a fascinating spectacle of the play of minds, each watching for a weakening in the other. Both, in their different ways, were obstinate men. Each remained firm on one essential point — Kang on British admission of responsibility; Kerans, acting at all times on the Commander-in-Chief's brief, on denial of it. Indeed, as we know, he was never authorised by Brind to negotiate on this point, but found himself forced into long and sterile arguments. Quite clearly, the British also had the strongest possible claim for 'responsibility' and 'compensation'; but Stevenson, behind the scenes, was rightly emphasising that this was not the time for the British, any more than the Communists, to raise this point. That would come later. The liberation of the ship, on purely military grounds, was the first point. Intense activity was going on behind the scenes. The Commander-in-Chief, without success, was trying to approach the Chinese Commander-in-Chief, General Chu Teh. Personal approaches were being attempted, such as that by Lieutenant-General Sir Adrian Carton de Wiart, VC, who, as Mr Churchill's personal representative, had been on good terms with Chou En-lai. None availed.

Soon, however, the word 'responsibility' began to fade as, under continued categorical denial, the Communists began to suggest other words which we might accept but which would still save their 'face'. In this dour battle there were sudden, swift reversals and changes of front, from a softening back to a hardening, from a thaw to a frost, with tempers frayed and on one occasion lost. Concessions promised at one meeting were taken away at the next and new and harsher demands made. There were occasionally discussions also on more immediate matters of *Amethyst's* pressing domestic needs, non-military needs that could easily be satisfied by the normal transaction of organised civilian life now largely restored; and on these, 'because the CPLA bears no ill-will' to the British ship, there was some slackening of Communist rigour. Concessions in these minor matters were useful opiates for keeping the victim hopeful of life and release until the next rebuff.

Kerans had no fewer than eleven meetings with Kang, on three of which Yuan was also present. Some were occupied merely in chewing over old rags, while Kang was trying by every means in his power to persuade or threaten Kerans into the vital damaging admission. The Communist had got his prisoner and was determined to wring from him a 'confession' of guilt. No confession, no liberty. There is no need to record all these meetings in detail, but the main line of them is an essential leading-up to the final act as well as being a revelation of the mind and method of the Communist — though Yuan and Kang were far from being exemplars of Communism at its worst.

These meetings were held in various places, sometimes at Chinkiang, sometimes in the more picturesque setting of Silver Island, sometimes in the squalid little village where Captain Tai, as Kang's watchdog, kept his baleful young eye upon the motionless ship. At these meetings Kerans, determined never again to go alone, adopted the excellent practice of taking one of the Petty Officers with him, in addition to Leo. He did this for three reasons — first, to give himself the comfort and confidence of having a fellow-countryman with him; second, as a means of giving the lower deck a more intimate appreciation of what was going on; and third, in case he himself should be 'liquidated'. In this way he took with him White, Frank, Williams, McCarthy, Freeman and Chare. Needless to say, the Petty Officers were delighted with the idea; it was a rare and choice experience for them and for Kerans it was a comfort to have a friend at hand.

In spite of the possibility of assassination, Kerans and his companions never went to these meetings armed. Their only weapon was the folder of papers which Kerans carried under his arm and which contained the brief he had carefully prepared for himself before each meeting. After the first Chinkiang meeting the ship's company changed into white tropical uniform, and Kerans always insisted that he and his companion should be impeccably turned out, however bad the weather. For, as the heat came, so also did the rains, and in the twenty minutes walk from river-side to distant road, through muddy paths and paddy fields, they were often soaked before they reached the car, adding to the discomfort of the long, wearying discussions. When the meetings were held in Chinkiang there was always this foot journey at the start and finish, with Tai always acting as escort in the command car. For the meetings on Silver Island, which were held in a building near the quay, with the fir woods and the temples spread serenely above them, a launch would be provided. When they met in the little village near the ship, of which no one ever seems certainly to have known the name, it was in a small farm of fairly good standard set within a courtyard of whitewashed stone walls in a bare, fairly clean room containing nothing but a table and chairs, and with the peasants kept carefully out of sight.

According to Chinese custom in hot weather, Kerans and his companion were given hot, clean towels on their arrival at meetings to wipe off the perspiration. They were also served with the pale, 'green' Chinese tea in little cups, kept constantly replenished by orderlies. Kang would occasionally nibble a melon seed from a dish on the table, and he and most of the other Chinese smoked incessantly. There were cigarettes on the table but Kerans used his own. What the Commissar never did was to smile. He had no sense of humour at all and his granite face never relaxed in its aspect of grim intensity beneath the cold stare of the monster photograph of Mao Tse-tung.

Kerans prepared for these meetings with the utmost care. Before every one he sat down in his cabin, sometimes far into the night, and prepared a brief for himself, first of all setting out the points of the Commander-in-Chief's instructions to him, then supplementing them with facts in support, listing, as far as he could anticipate them, the arguments that Kang might bring out, and weighing up the order and manner in which he would present his case, keeping in reserve those points in which the Commander-in-Chief had given him discretion. He had to do all his own typing, and on one occasion an angry Kang exclaimed that his little typing errors were an 'insult' to the CPLA.

At the second meeting, held in the village on the last day of May, battle was waged over a factual account of the Rose Island engagement that the Commander-in-Chief himself had signalled and that Kerans had sent on to Kang. The Commissar, though he quite obviously knew only half the story, 'constantly refuted and disbelieved all facts concerning the incident... he would not deviate from his attitude of complete negation.' From this fruitless wrangle, however, there came an interesting revelation. What, asked Kerans towards the end of it, was Kang's evidence for his charge that *Amethyst* fired first?

'Because,' said the Commissar, 'I commanded the battery on San Chiang Ying and personally witnessed the whole thing. I had ordered my troops not to fire unless fired on first, and therefore there is no doubt that you fired first.'

'That is an extremely weak answer and no evidence,' answered Kerans.

Kang dropped the subject at once and never raised it again. It then dawned on Kerans that Kang Mao-chao and the phonetic 'Major Kung', whom Freeman and Hett had seen at the beginning, but whom Kerans himself never saw, were one and the same person. Of course! he said to himself, that explains the whole thing. Kang's superiors had clearly said 'You've got us into this mess; now you get us out.' It explained also the revival of 'Kang's' bogus 'first shot'.

June came in blazing and humid, and in the next three weeks there was a series of stiff and arid meetings in which Kang used every artifice of pressure or persuasion to force Kerans to assume responsibility on all counts and to admit primary guilt; without which, he said icily, *Amethyst* could not be released. Kerans categorically refused and stuck grimly to his guns, his brief and the simple facts. Granite met granite. He knew well that the Communists' tactics would be to wear him out by attrition and that, in Stevenson's words, his best defence was 'patience, determination and good temper'; though good temper was hard to maintain when the Commissar insulted the Commander-in-Chief by doubting his good faith.

The only practical progress made in all these three weeks was to win permission for Leo to go to Nanking to bring back from the Embassy some of the new Communist 'People's Money' (*Jen min piao*) with which to buy provisions. Scarcely less valuable was a letter he brought from the Ambassador of warm praise and encouragement. 'I can assure you,' Stevenson wrote, 'that we are doing our damnedest to try and effect your release from an intolerable position... I am deeply impressed by the admirable manner in which you have been handling a very difficult situation.'

The Commander-in-Chief sent a like message. Reporting to him a particularly hopeless meeting, Kerans ended: *Rest assured, sir, that all on board are determined to hold out come what may.* To which, Brind, now about to return to Hong Kong, replied: *I entirely approve your conduct of negotiations and am proud of the spirit and determination of all in the* Amethyst.

Such genuine recognition was just what was badly needed by a young captain to sustain him in a time of severe trial, strain and self-questioning. Acutely aware as he was of his heavy responsibility, and conscious that he was up against an opponent highly skilled in all the arts of hard bargaining, it is inevitable that he should often have felt desperately lonely and that he should sometimes ask himself whether he had the ability and strength to see the thing through.

His firm stand seemed likely to be rewarded and a new hope dawned when, to his relief, he met Yuan himself on June 20th. Yuan had clearly been taken by surprise by the narration of events that Brind had sent to him, and he was at first in an indignant mood. Why, the rotund little General wanted to know, had *Amethyst* been sent to relieve *Consort* when it must have been realised that Nanking was about to fall? Here, he said, spreading them out on the table and reading some of them, are plenty of Press extracts reporting numerous crossings of the Yangtse and bombardments between April 19th and 20th in the Chinkiang area. This was, in fact, about the only fair and relevant question on the whole subject that Yuan or Kang ever asked. It was really the kernel of the whole thing, but as far as the Press extracts were concerned Kerans was able to denounce them promptly as worthless.

'I was present myself,' he said icily, 'the whole of the night of April 21st-22nd, in the areas said to have been occupied by your troops, and I know they are not true.'

Press evidence was never again mentioned.

Why, Yuan wanted to know next, had the other ships, *London*, *Black Swan* and *Consort*, been sent into the area to add to the 'infringement of Chinese sovereignty' already committed by *Amethyst*?

'Because,' said Kerans, 'you yourselves tried to destroy one of His Majesty's ships on a peaceful mission. The other ships came on a humanitarian task of rescue, intending to tow *Amethyst* out of the Yangtse. We tried to get away from what you claim to have been your territory, but you would not let us.'

It was quite apparent that the Communists had only a partial knowledge of the facts and that Brind's narration of the actual events had upset them. Yuan was very irritable. The 'people of China', he said, were 'indignant' about the whole incident. And as for Kerans himself — 'You have prevaricated and delayed everything and Colonel Kang has been unable to settle anything with you.'

Curious arguments. *Amethyst* was hardly the party that had any interest in delaying matters. However, these arguments led up to something constructive and full of new hope. Calming down, Yuan presently made a hopeful suggestion. If, he said, the Commander-in-Chief would respect facts and acknowledge the basic faults of *intrusion* and *infringement* of Chinese territorial waters, then he, Yuan, might consider a separate solution for the release of *Amethyst* and the continuation of discussions on questions of apology and compensation.

Here was encouragement. Here was a less rigid outlook. 'Intrusion' and 'infringement' were something very different from 'invasion' and 'brutal acts'. Kerans felt that this went a long way towards finding a compromise formula. Yuan concluded by saying that he was anxious for an early solution of the problem and for *Amethyst* to be enabled to rejoin the Fleet. He expressed regret at the inconveniences being suffered by the ship and specially enjoined Kerans to convey his regrets to Brind. This more reasonable attitude was perhaps due, not only to Yuan's different training and outlook, for he was of an older school than Kang, but also to the efforts that were being made on the political level behind the scenes.

Two days later Kerans was surprised to see Yuan himself again; he came in unexpectedly at a discussion with Kang about the admission of the ship's mail and supplies, and at once resumed the major issue. He repeated his wish for a peaceful settlement and said now that this could best be done by an *exchange of notes at his level*, not Kang's. The British, he now said, should:

> Acknowledge the BASIC facts that a British warship (singular) had INTRUDED INDISCREETLY into the CPLA Frontier Area without their permission; and
> Give assurances that negotiations would be continued later.

'Do you consider this method reasonable?' Yuan asked.

'Yes, I do; but I repeat that it is not in my province to negotiate on the first point at this stage.'

He was very much encouraged, observing that Yuan was prepared to adopt methods of diplomacy, instead of the Molotov methods of Kang. He was prepared, it seemed, to negotiate a settlement instead of imposing one. The really important things in this new formula were the omissions of 'provocation', 'invasion', apologies' and 'compensation' as essential admissions before safe conduct. Yuan seemed genuinely worried over the hardships and inconveniences now being suffered by the ship's company, which we shall see for ourselves very soon, and for this reason he gave his official clearance then and there for the early entry of the ship's mail from Shanghai.

Alas, however, this was, in Kerans's words, 'the last hopeful meeting' that took place.

CHAPTER 12: THE CAPTIVE SHIP

IT WAS now nearly the end of June and *Amethyst* had been bottled up for more than two months. All that time she had had no replenishments of any sort except the small amounts of vegetables bartered at a hard price or bought with People's Money from the Nanking Embassy, itself now living a strained and thorny existence. The ship was living entirely 'on her fat', such as she had left. She was being deliberately denied perfectly normal facilities which, the war having moved far on, had long since been readily available to the general community — transport, the delivery of goods, mail and all the normal transactions of organised life. For all these things she had to ask permission, though the meanest coolie could send and receive letters, the smallest business despatch and receive goods by train or sea. No communications whatever with the outside world had been permitted except by wireless or by Leo's occasional, somewhat risky trips to Nanking. Miss Dunlap, who always remained a friend of *Amethyst*, attempted to visit the ship, but was turned back at the bayonet point and was told by the Communists that they would keep the ship there until the men on board 'starved to death'. No mail had been allowed in, no oil, no stores, no disinfectants or medical supplies, except, again, a small consignment of penicillin sent by Donaldson by hand of Leo. The sun's steepening rays grew daily fiercer, the humidity more and more dense. Drenching rains fell like sheets of water, beating on the steel ship with metallic throb. High winds and sudden storms turned the Yangtse into an angry sea and shook the lightly laden frigate at her anchorage like a leaf in a summer gale. The waters, fed by the heavy rains and the melting mountain snows far inland, swelled and rose, rushing past the ship at the rate of five knots. The rats multiplied and began to invade all parts of the ship. A plague of cockroaches spread. Ants swarmed. Myriads of mosquitoes and all the queer flying insects of a tropical wet season infested the ship. The south-west monsoon had begun.

Most serious of all the shortages was fuel oil. At Rose Island on April 20th *Amethyst* had had in her tanks 365 tons of fuel oil and fourteen tons of diesel (which can also be used for the main engines if necessary, one ton of diesel being equivalent to half a ton of furnace oil). With the hope of an early release, auxiliary steam had been kept up on the normal economy standards and the ship had been using 6.6 tons of oil a day. But on May 20th Kerans began to be worried. On that day he was down to 170 tons plus nine tons of diesel. Out of that he must set aside thirty tons[10] for his passage down-river — whenever, and if ever, that took place. He had, therefore, at that rate of consumption, sufficient oil for only another twenty-six days, after which the ship would become immobile. In the present bleak outlook of the wrangles with Kang, there seemed small prospect of a release by that time.

He therefore began a long and exacting course of fuel economy, the first step of which, with the approval of Madden (who, remember, had administrative charge), was to shut down all electric power completely for twelve hours each night. This reduced the oil expenditure to three tons a day, providing for the distillation of fresh water, ventilation, the cooling of the ammunition magazines, the main wireless, the refrigerators and the pumping out of compartments. The immediate and more

---

[10] Approximately sixteen tons of this had to be allowed for 'loss of suction' — that quantity of oil in the tanks which was below the outlet pipes when the ship was on an even keel.

palpable effects, however, were that all ventilating fans stopped at night and there was no electric light, except for a few dim pinpoints in essential places from emergency batteries. A stiffing, stagnant, humid atmosphere was built up below decks. As the weather gradually grew hotter, and the humidity more oppressive, sleep became virtually impossible and all who could do so came up and slept on the upper deck until driven down by torrential rain. All torch batteries had long ago been exhausted and even the anchor light was a mere candle in an improvised lantern, so that twice the ship was nearly run down at night. To maintain wireless communication when power was shut down, the main W/T set was replaced by the battery-operated Type 60 set, which just managed to last long enough.

This predicament was reported to Kang at that time, but it was a matter he did not understand, for, as we know, for a long time he thought the ship was fired by coal. He cross-examined Kerans on matters of fuel consumption and how things worked, but was kept in the dark. Kerans was good at that. A little later he guardedly gave a date in early July as the time when fuel would be exhausted and the ship immobile. On June 3rd stocks were down to 136 tons, furnace and diesel. Every day the consumption figures were marked up to two places of decimals on a blackboard in Kerans's cabin, together with those for the stocks of food. Further economy had been effected by isolating one engine completely, and the distillation of fresh water was considerably reduced.

By June 15th supplies were down to 106 tons and consumption was still further reduced by shutting down for complete twenty-four hour periods. This was a very bad patch, for the weather was abominable, with almost continual rain, and the damp heat below, in which men seemed to be drained of energy, became hard to bear. For no one was this state of affairs worse than for the engine-room department. During the shut-down periods, with no fans going, the machinery spaces became virtually untenable and, when the time came for 'flashing-up' again, almost unapproachable. As the inspecting officers at Hong Kong said later, it was 'only by sheer guts', that the thing was done.

A week later (June 22nd), however, Kerans took the still more drastic step of shutting down all power for periods of two and a half days (actually fifty-nine hours) at a stretch, thus reducing consumption to only one ton per day. Life in the suffocating ship became more and more forbidding. The fresh water sparingly made in the few hours of running was carefully hoarded. What there was had to be carried or hand-pumped, for all power pumps ceased. There was no pressure to flush the 'heads' and men were therefore obliged to use the side of the ship. Throughout the ship all machinery was silenced and the familiar undertones of ship's life gave place to an eerie quiet in which all human sounds echoed as in a steel vault. *Amethyst* was a 'dead' ship.

All hands, knowing these things had to be done, bore the hardships cheerfully, though continuously dissolving in perspiration and drained of strength. The only signs of strain, said Fearnley, were a few gastric upsets. These youngsters from the distant city streets of home had not the slightest intention of giving way to the oppressions of the Commissar, of whose manoeuvres they were kept continuously informed, and their high spirit was the measure not only of their native courage but also of the fine leadership of officers and petty officers.

At the meeting with Kang on June 22nd — the meeting at which Yuan unexpectedly turned up — Kerans fought to get these hardships reduced. He asked for the ship's mail to be allowed through, and whether clearance could be given for a merchant ship to come in with the various stores and supplies so urgently needed. There could hardly, he supposed, be any objection to a merchant ship, for the Yangtse had been declared open to merchant shipping, and vessels of every kind were daily making passage up and down. Yuan, however, categorically refused. It was, he said, a most 'improper' suggestion — an 'infringement of Chinese territorial waters'. It did not, apparently, occur to him that there was no 'infringement' when permission was asked and granted.

Kerans countered him by saying that the requirement was entirely due to the Communists' own action and that this was the least that he could do to alleviate the hardships of the ship's company. Above all, he said, the need for fuel had now become critical; if the Communists really meant what they said about not wishing the ship's company to endure hardships, they could not possibly refuse them fuel. The matter was perfectly easy. Through the long-term foresight of the Naval Attaché, the Royal Navy had itself carefully built up a reserve for emergencies at Hogee, outside Nanking, by contributions from the visiting guard-ships. It was the Navy's own oil, all in drums. It would be a simple matter, said Kerans, to send that down-river. Yuan said coldly that he would consider an application if made in writing, and a week later Tai came on board to say that the request had been granted.

In the next week, so rigid was the economy, only five tons were used. Then came a period in the general negotiations in which the Communists' attitude assumed a new note of hostile asperity and intransigence, and Kerans was informed that the Hogee fuel would now be stopped. All on board were in low spirits. There seemed to be no hope anywhere. What would be the Communists' next move? On July 9th, total oil supplies were down to 62.7 tons.

But the fuel came. Late on July 9th, having been warned, hands were looking up-river and presently they saw a small tug towing an enormous lighter. This was it. Everyone watched fascinated and amused as the little tug, grossly underpowered and inefficiently handled, struggled with the rapid tide to bring her great burden in on the port side of the frigate — only to ground on a sandbank. A frenzied altercation took place between the tug and the local garrison, whose orders were to permit no ship to approach the *Amethyst*, but at last the precious cargo was secured alongside. It had arrived only in the nick of time, for that same evening the battery-driven wireless set broke down, the last and only valve for it having given out. That meant that in future they could communicate with the outside world only when the engines were 'flashed up'.

It was too late to start taking on the oil that night with safety, but at five next morning every officer and rating in the ship, except the captain and the cooks, turned out stripped to the waist. There were 294 drums to take on, empty and return to the junk. They were hoisted on board by tackle at the davit heads, rolled to all three fuelling connections and there drained into the tanks; on the forward fuelling position a semi-rotary pump and hoses were rigged, and on the other two the drums were rolled up wooden ramps and emptied by funnels. The operation was carried out with an efficiency, energy and cheerfulness that did the heart good to see — 'everyone working like hell,' as Coxswain Frank said, 'to get the job finished as soon as possible, oil all over the place, everyone covered in the stuff, but no one cares.' Working non-stop for eleven hours under the sweltering July sun, drenched with perspiration and with oil, kept going by frequent draughts of lime juice, hands finished the job by four in the afternoon, having added a priceless fifty-four tons to the tanks, making now a total of 116 tons. They had taken only eleven hours to do the job instead of a calculated twenty-two. It was an astonishing feat and one, thought Frank, 'without parallel in the history of our Navy'; and he added: 'What makes this all the more praiseworthy is that not only have the ship's company had no exercise for eighty-two days, but also everything used in the operation had to be improvised.'

For this fifty-four tons of the Royal Navy's own oil the Communists charged the equivalent of £400 for 'delivery'.

All were elated, but they had not yet learned the ways of Communism. An easing of the strain was bound to import a fresh hardening. The concession of the oil was followed the very next day by a meeting of violent hostility with Kang. Further replenishment of all sorts was refused, everything was refused, and Kerans was subjected to personal abuse. Accompanied this time by Strain, he came back to the ship looking very serious, mustered all hands and said: 'Tomorrow we go on half rations.'

There was a deathly silence. 'Throughout the ship,' said Frank, 'you could have heard a pin drop.'

Kang, instead of growing more reasonable as time went on, was putting the screw on harder and harder. He saw the ship at his mercy and resolved to beat her into subjection. He could not see, however, what Frank wrote in his diary that night:

> Kang does not know the British sailor, and whatever the Captain decides, he can rest assured that we are all with him, and we shall not let him down.

For the food situation was now as serious as the oil situation had been. Indeed, had the ship not been ninety-seven hands short, there would by now have been no food at all. Stocks of frozen meat were very low and all other supplies were gradually running out. There was enough flour to last only till the end of the month — another twenty days. There was still some soap and clothing for bartering with the local villain if their small supply of money ran out, but after that there would be nothing. Even the sheets of toilet paper had to be cut in halves and later halved again.

The rats, too, were hungry. Probably they had come on board at Hong Kong or Shanghai, and undoubtedly they had been shaken out of their hiding places by the shelling. They soon spread to all parts of the ship in the search for food that was now so scarce. Their nails scratched the steel decks all night and their sharp squeals sounded behind all bulkheads. They invaded the mess-decks, they penetrated the bread lockers, they ate the books in the wardroom, they ran across men as they slept. The encroached on the upper deck and even invaded the sanctity of the bridge. The adults were big rats, bigger than Simon, the little cat that hunted them. Every device was used against them. Some fifty or sixty traps were made, but ship's rats are particularly wily creatures and very few fell to the snares. Simon was the more efficient, but he was heavily outnumbered and the dog Peggy was not interested. Towards the end, however, the vermin seemed to decrease in number, or to withdraw, for the ship was left so clean and precautions were so strict that there was little for them to eat. But while they lasted they were certainly an enemy in the nerve war, for rats in large numbers do not compose the imagination or induce the mind to easy sleep.

For two months, in spite of repeated requests, the ship's company received no home mail, that precious commodity to the Serviceman abroad. As the result of Yuan's promise of June 20th, however, three bags of it arrived at Chinkiang Post Office four days later. It was obtained, however, only by the most persistent efforts by Leo and the Chinese Leading Cook, who was given this task as an opportunity for a spell ashore. At the Post Office every possible barrier was put in their way by both military and postal officials. The mail had left Shanghai unsealed on Shanghai's orders but Chinkiang refused to hand it over because it was *not* sealed. It was seen also by the condition of the letters that both ends had had a go not only at censoring but also at pilfering. From then on, with the exception of the fuel, Kang took an increasing part in hindering the entry of anything into *Amethyst*.

There was great rejoicing on board at the receipt of the mail, but outward mail was forbidden. However, there was one way out of this — the wireless. During the course of the captivity the unwearying French sent out over 250 personal messages which were picked up the other end and delivered to relatives as telegrams, to be paid for later. At home the Admiralty also co-operated by circulating news to all next-of-kin.

The sun daily increased in severity, shortly to reach its climax. On the upper deck the steel — and most things were of steel — burnt the hand. The deck itself was far too hot to walk about on with bare feet, or to sit upon. A tropical routine was worked, from daylight till 12.30 pm, after which hands were free for the rest of the day and wore the flimsiest and the most informal clothing. Indeed, as Fearnley said afterwards, sometimes they looked like a gang of pirates. Day and night in the humid atmosphere men streamed with perspiration. Sound sleep became impossible to most men and was vicariously substituted by an unquiet tossing about all night, virtually naked. In the wireless office Blomley or Rutter blew air by a hand bellows on to French as he worked his set. Below decks the thermometer reached 100 degrees and the bulkheads streamed with moisture. The whole ship was hot, damp and suffocating.

Yet the health and spirits of the men remained high and buoyant. The lack of shore contacts, the good food and the strict hygiene on board were the chief promoters of this excellent condition, though hands, it is true, had to be constantly 'chased' about flushing the 'heads' at night with Yangtse water. The good food and the lack of exercise caused many of the ship's company, especially Fearnley and Frank, to grow fat. French contracted 'athlete's foot', or something of the sort, from his persistent use of gym shoes in spite of repeated advice. Some house flies reached the ship but there was only one case of dysentery, apart from mild 'tummy troubles' of the sort usually experienced in tropical climates. With the shore only 500 yards away, swarms of mosquitoes invaded the ship in June, the worst sufferers being the officers and ratings who frequented the W/T office, and in order to obtain identifications, Fearnley issued them with test tubes and asked them to collect specimens. 'They co-operated enthusiastically,' he said, 'and the next morning I was presented with a large collection of blood-engorged female mosquitoes.' They proved to be the infective sorts of anopheles, but malaria was kept entirely at bay by the daily tablet of mepacrine, or of Paludrine, when it arrived later.

Far more medically 'interesting' for Fearnley than this bunch of fit young fellows were the Chinese, whom he got permission from Kerans to treat. It all began with the women of the sampan 'side-party'. One day 'Cheesi' brought her eighteen-months-old baby to Fearnley and asked for his help. Thick yellow pus was discharging from the child's left eye. Fearnley, diagnosing conjunctivitis, gave penicillin and other treatments and in a few days the child was cured.

Fearnley was, so to speak, a made man. His next applicant was one of the contractors, who, said the young doctor, 'had not led a blameless life'. He proved to be a stubborn case, and received treatment for several weeks. A steady trail of villagers and fishermen then began to come out to the ship until, on account of the shortage of drugs, it had to be ordered that only the relatives of the sampan women would be treated.

It may be hoped that these ministrations did something material towards fostering the 'Sino-British friendship' that Kang was so fond of talking about, but when it was *Amethyst* herself that needed medical help the response was neither prompt nor enthusiastic. Boy First Glass Sidney Horton, a lad of seventeen, injured his right arm on June 5th and Fearnley suspected a fracture of the humerus. An X-ray photograph was therefore to be desired and a request was made to Kang for this facility at a Chinkiang hospital, but it was fifteen days before he was allowed to go, by which time the swelling had almost disappeared and partial use of the arm recovered. It would, of course, have been bad propaganda to have sent the boy to the Goldsby King Mission Hospital, and he and Fearnley were accordingly taken by jeep on June 20th to a hospital under Communist control.

'There was,' said Fearnley afterwards, 'a distinct lack of ordinary medical courtesy and the taking of the X-ray was obviously considered an imposition. The standard of medical education may be gauged by the fact that one of the medical students, when he learnt that a simple crack fracture of more than two weeks' duration was to be excluded, asked the boy if he had any fever, and seemed disappointed when the reply was in the negative.

'Finally the X-ray department was reached, where it was considered necessary to screen first. This of course produced no information beyond the fact that an elbow joint with the usual number of bones was present... A plate was then taken. The most important part of the whole procedure was the bill, which was presented to me almost immediately.'

A plate of poor clarity arrived four days later.

Thus in their health and their spirits the ship's company won a battle against the conditions that threatened to oppress them. As far as those conditions allowed, a normal life and routine continued to be followed, and a proper and a willing discipline was easily maintained. 'Captain's Rounds', when the ship is inspected, took place every Saturday as usual, and Church service every Sunday. Strain, in his broad Scots, was always in the van in keeping up a cheerful heart, and Hett's quiet, unflurried manner was a fortifying influence. Men's minds were kept as busy as possible. When electric power was provided the seven motion pictures that the ship carried were put on the screen — till all hands knew each of them by heart! A small stock of gramophone records, played over the ship's internal broadcast system, did something to distract from the humid heat. Kerans did not believe in 'organised games' run by officers and thought it better for hands to run their own, which they did very successfully. Mercifully, the Naafi stocks of cigarettes, ice cream and other material comforts held out. They were issued by Macnamara on a credit basis and in the course of time Naafi did not forget to present their bills, though the officers were generously excused the greater part of their bill for wines (much of which had been lost in the Rose Island shelling) by the directors of Galdbeck & McGregor at Hong Kong.

A different kind of reckoning was to be settled soon, however, for the days were fast running out.

CHAPTER 13: THE SCREW IS TIGHTENED

THE Commander-in-Chief was quick to reply to Yuan's promising new formula of June 22nd. The General's suggestions, he said, were welcomed as providing a basis for an agreed statement of *mutual* rights and the quick release of *Amethyst*. Kerans hurried off a memorandum to Kang and sent Leo with it.

Kang, at the next meeting, however, at once objected to the word 'mutual' and this was the beginning of a lengthy harangue for some weeks over exact Chinese transliterations. A day or two later Brind, who was, of course, keeping watchful liaison in all these matters with the Ambassador and the Admiralty, signalled the actual wording that he suggested for the exchange of notes of which Yuan had spoken. As this was the basis of subsequent terminological battles, and as it shows how much Brind was prepared to meet Yuan without dishonour, this short draft is worth recording in detail:

1. I am very glad to hear that you are prepared to grant a safe-passage down the Yangtse river for HMS *Amethyst* and I formally ask that this may be given.
2. I recognise that HMS *Amethyst* [unfortunately] entered the China People's Liberation Army's Frontier Zone without the concurrence of the command of the China People's Liberation Army.
3. I am sure you will share my very deep regret at the casualties caused on both sides.
4. This message is without prejudice to subsequent negotiations which will take place later by our superior

authorities. I give you my assurance that there will be no objections by the British side to these negotiations taking place.

Kerans sent this off at once to Kang, but, under the discretion given to him by Brind, omitted the word 'unfortunately'. He thought there was a possibility that the Chinese characters for it might be associated with a sense of guilt. A spell of very bad weather followed, with high winds, lashing rain and rough water, in which it was impossible for the sampan women to make the passage between ship and shore, and during which Kerans was laid up with a bad attack of fibrositis brought on by the damp heat of the ship and by the soakings that he got on his visits ashore. As he lay in his bunk, he received instructions from Brind to avoid the use of any adverb or adjective in place of 'unfortunately', if he could; but if obliged, he was to use the following, in order of preference: 'at an unfortunate moment', 'unfortunate', 'imprudent', 'indiscreet'. Such was the hair-splitting the huckstering in words, to which they had descended! But Brind added humanly: *They certainly seem trying hard to get you down. Good luck.*

Well, here was a pretty sort of lawyer's business for a simple naval officer to get mixed up with! It was, after all, a lawyer with whom he had to negotiate — a lawyer crafty and fanatical. Ill and debilitated by the humid heat, perplexed enough about the maintenance of the ship's life and being, Kerans felt keenly the need for an experienced mind at his side — someone versed in the ways of diplomacy and who understood the Chinese mind and the finer points of its language. He thought of Teddy Youde at the Nanking Embassy and wondered whether there was a chance that Kang would let him in. Leo was intelligent but Kerans felt the need for someone who could put himself in his own shoes, who understood the finer points involved and who could help him share the burden. But Kerans knew by now that Kang did not want a trained mind on the scene; he preferred to deal with the simple sailor. So, for the time being, Kerans knew that he would have to struggle on alone, doing his best 'to negotiate himself out', but always keeping certain things hidden in the secrecy of his own mind.

All the end of June and early July was a very bad time. The weather was exceedingly rough. High winds howled across the Yangtse and the rain fell like a waterfall. Keeping watch on the bridge was an ordeal, but scarcely more of an ordeal than to be driven below into the steamy and oppressive atmosphere. 'Things,' said Frank, 'were beginning to get grim.' By night he listened to the distant roar of the legions of frogs and the unceasing call of the cuckoo. By day the whole landscape shimmered in the sun, the horizon dancing on the waves of heat and the distant ships in the river appearing to sail in the air. The cockroaches, undeterred by DDT, the ants and the mosquitoes multiplied and swarmed. A Chinese hand, his gear crawling with cockroaches, was discovered trying to smuggle drugs. Large passenger and cargo vessels were now passing freely up and down the Yangtse and one of them anchored abreast of the *Amethyst* for a night. Ships began to pay her the accustomed courtesy of the sea, dipping their ensigns as they passed. The smallest incident was a relief to the stifling monotony.

For the first week of July all the local Communist leaders went off for seven days of 'victory celebrations' in Nanking, and Kerans was told by Tai Kuo-liang that there was no chance of any further meeting with Kang until they were all over. The added delay was exasperating, for Kerans felt, after his last talk with Yuan, that negotiations up till now had gone a long way towards clearing the ground, and no hint of any

194

major obstacle was given. It appeared that the choice of the exact words of the notes was all that now stood in the way of the ship's freedom.

'This,' he said afterwards, 'was a depressing period and personally my spirits were low, as I did not see what I could do next — and time was vital. The inactivity was beginning to tell on us all.'

Small reliefs came, however, and on July 1st they got in a small quantity of urgent stores from Shanghai. Khoong Chung-tsung, chief driver and trusted emissary of Pringle, the Assistant Naval Attaché there, with great initiative and boldness, managed to get through by train up to Chinkiang after a very difficult journey, during which he was twice closely interrogated and within an ace of being arrested. But Khoong was no ordinary person. Short and broad, he was a cheerful soul who faced obstacles with a strong determination and a persuasive smile. By arrangement, Leo and the Chinese Leading Cook went to meet him and brought back some letters, medical stores, mosquito netting and People's Money that Khoong had delivered to them. Khoong had also brought up for them some new Chinese charts of the Lower Yangtse, but these the CPLA confiscated, although they had been paid for in a Chinese shop and the receipt was shown to them. These, said the Communists, were 'secret', having been issued by the 'reactionary Kuomintang government'. No amount of remonstrance would persuade them otherwise. The real reason for their confiscation was that the CPLA thought that *Amethyst* might need them for an escape. There is no doubt but that Kang thought to the end that she could not get away without them. Kerans let him go on thinking so, taking every opportunity of complaining bitterly.

At the same time Kerans noted with interest that the movement of shipping in the river by night was permitted and evidently feasible. This night movement indicated that control of shipping had been relaxed and that passage past Kiang Yin could not be so very difficult. Far away, Brind's Staff Officer Intelligence had also made a significant mental note of the same fact when Kerans had reported that he had been twice nearly run down by merchant ships that could not see his feeble anchor-light candle.

Immediately after the Nanking victory junketings Kerans received a summons to meet Kang in the adjacent village of uncertain name. He went with alacrity, and again 'Midnight' and 'Granny' rowed him ashore over the fast-rushing waters in a heavy downpour of rain. He paused before going only to type a formal application for the admission of Youde as an additional interpreter. On this occasion he took Frank with him, and the ship's company watched them go in the lashing rain with high expectations, for in the whole of this period since Yuan's formula of June 22nd it had appeared to everyone that a reasoned diplomacy had now replaced the concrete front of Kang. Kerans and Frank splashed through the mud to the small farm and began the meeting in a state of acute physical discomfort, but hopeful of an atmosphere less barbed with thorns and briars than before. They were immediately disabused. Kang demanded fundamental and damaging changes in the Commander-in-Chief's draft note. The British had to admit having 'infringed into China's national river' and to committing 'a basic fault'. The article on mutual regrets for casualties had to be struck out altogether, and Article 4 had to promise to discuss 'apologies and compensation'.

None of the qualifying adjectives that Kerans had been given discretion to use was acceptable. They were back where they had been before the meeting with Yuan. Kang, the black beads of his eyes glinting with concentration, beat hard to break in the doors of Kerans's resistance and batter him into accepting 'invasion' again and such terms as 'fundamental guilt', and it was useless to point out to him that all this vitiated Yuan's proposals of June 22nd, that admission of guilt could not precede inquiry, and that such inquiry must be on a diplomatic level.

This was not at all hopeful, and still less hopeful was an entirely diversionary trick that Kang sprang on the astonished Kerans. Who, he asked, was authorised to negotiate amendments, present and sign this note when it was agreed?

'I am, of course. You have seen the authorisation,' Kerans answered.

'That was only a wireless message. General Yuan will require it to be in writing.'

'In writing! That is impossible. You allow us no contact with the Fleet and the Admiral is in Japan.'

This was a surprise to Kang. 'Nevertheless,' he said, 'if it is not in writing, it cannot be legal.' This was after negotiations had been going on for over two months!

Nor was any progress made in the simple affair of Youde's entry. Finally the matter of the confiscated charts was raised, but Kerans, the perspiration streaming from him, met only a stone wall of indifference and was so exasperated that he lost his temper.

'I must have them,' he said. 'How the hell do you think all these other ships go up and down the river?'

'When you go, you will be provided with a pilot.'

'I shall still need the charts, and so will the pilot.'

Kang had not seen, as we have seen, nor was he disabused, that Kerans had already brought on board a set of Chinese

Admiralty charts from Rose Island onwards; he lacked only the section of chart from the ship's present position as far as the island.

It was all very instructive for Frank, who records Kerans's anger when one of the Commissar's interpreters was caught by Leo giving a false translation and how 'the captain threw down his pencil and told the Commissar's party what he thought of them in good plain English'.

At this moment Geoffrey Weston re-enters the story for a fleeting moment, in an audacious and nearly successful attempt to rejoin his ship, one that was to be frustrated by that long sequence of mischances that dogged the frigate for so long.

Weston, having got a satisfactory 'chop' from the doctors in Shanghai after quitting Nanking, soon began to fret. 'I felt,' he said, 'as Uriah felt at the siege of Rabbah' — being kept out of his comrade's battle.

Kerans, on returning from his stormy meeting with Kang on July 5th, received a signal from Pringle in Shanghai, to say that the Communist police had ordered Weston to leave Shanghai within twenty-four hours and that he was accordingly being sent to rejoin his ship. Kerans therefore sent Leo ashore with a letter informing Kang.

On the evening of the 7th Weston left Shanghai, properly authorised by a pass issued by the police, accompanied by the resourceful Khoong and carrying between them two suitcases full of cigarettes, sweets, soap and other stores. At Shanghai station the police thoroughly searched his person, ransacked his suitcases and read all his letters and papers, which were all fortunately harmless. Travelling all night, Weston and Khoong arrived at Chinkiang at 5.30 am next morning but were stopped by sentries from leaving the station. 'They took me,' reported Weston, 'to an office where I argued for a few hours with Communist officers. They said that my pass was not in order and out of date, that Lieutenant-Commander Kerans had not applied for permission for me to board, and that it was an "insult to Chinese National Sovereignty" that I should travel on Chinese National soil, and so on. I was able to prove the fallacy of their first two arguments but their other points were academic. However, they said they would convene a meeting of the *soi-disant* "*Amethyst* Committee" to consider the matter and returned to say that I was to go straight back to Shanghai without leaving the station.'

The Shanghai police had not informed the CPLA and Kang was coldly furious; it was probably due to this incident that the Commissar revoked the promise he had verbally given to admit Youde and that he delayed the Hogee oil for *Amethyst*.

It was on the day after the oil had arrived — on July 11th — that another crucial meeting took place. This time it was at the Chinkiang headquarters again and this time, because of the factors involved, Kerans took Strain with him. For this meeting Kerans had ready a new draft note from the Commander-in-Chief, designed by Brind to go as far as he could to meet the Communist view. Together with this Kerans was armed with a signalled authorisation for him to sign this final exchange note on the Commander-in-Chief's behalf. He had also a sharp personal letter from Brind — the sharpest he had yet sent — for Yuan personally, to be used at Kerans's discretion. Kerans was resolved, if he possibly could, to resume discussions with Yuan personally and to have as little as possible to do with Kang, whose behaviour and methods were a barrier to any agreement.

The meeting, however, hardly opened as Kerans had expected. It began with a tirade of abuse about Weston's arrival, all the blame for which was put on Kerans's shoulders. For about forty minutes Kerans listened to a stream of abuse of his actions in the past, even minor typing errors being considered as derogatory to the CPLA. Never had he been so 'bethumped with words'.

Kerans kept his temper and made no comment at all on this tirade, but, as soon as he could get in a word, handed in the Commander-in-Chief's new draft and for three hours all the old arguments were gone over again. Kang rejected this draft too and likewise refused to accept Brind's authorisation of Kerans unless it was in the Admiral's personal signature — to make it 'legal'. He could offer no suggestions of how, with the cutting off of the outside world that the CPLA had imposed, a personally signed letter could physically reach Chinkiang from Japan or Hong Kong or anywhere else. He also now demanded, as yet a further new point (there was always some new point to impose a fresh delay), that *London*, *Consort* and *Black Swan* should be specifically included as culprits in the incident, together with a return to 'apologies and compensation'. The whole business was put even further back than it had been in the very beginning of things.

Meeting this concrete wall of obstruction and plangent abuse, Kerans then brought up his reserve artillery and read out the personal letter from Brind to Yuan which he had received by signal. In this Brind said:

> I am not only disappointed but also extremely angry at the way *Amethyst's* ship's company is being treated… British officers and men in HMS *Amethyst* are now *being treated worse than the Japanese treated their prisoners of war…* I request your

200

support in overcoming all delays and in making immediate arrangements to replenish the ship and refresh her crew.

Kang sat like a stone. This straight speaking was not to his liking, especially the comparison with Japanese methods, which he declared to be a 'threat' to the CPLA. His voice took on a more menacing tone as he made it clear that neither ship nor aircraft would be allowed to approach *Amethyst* with supplies. Throughout the meeting the ship was constantly threatened with destruction if movement was attempted. Kerans's constant insistence that he could never be empowered to discuss high-level matters such as 'responsibility' for a 'guilty act' was met by the frigid answer that, unless he did, no progress would be made.

This was the worst meeting that Kerans had endured. The air was full of vitriol and heavy with evil purpose. A virtual ultimatum was delivered to submit to the Commissar's demands, and harsh, black-browed threats delivered to intensify the isolation of the ship and the severity of living conditions on board. Both Kerans and Strain could feel that further intimidations were clearly soon to be made.

It was after this black meeting that Kerans put the ship on half rations.

Amethyst's Captain had now come to the conclusion that the Communists' attitude might at any time change to one of immediate physical threats. Further supplies of fuel and food could no longer be relied upon. Before considering any positive action himself, however, he must reassure himself from the Commander-in-Chief on two points: (a) would a breaking-off of negotiations be acceptable politically or might it have unhappy repercussions on British communities elsewhere in China? and (b) if he attempted a break-out, would the loss of life that might result be acceptable?

Without any secure means of signalling, it was hard to put this across to the Commander-in-Chief. There was, however, one occurrence that might give him a chance to slip away; if a typhoon, the season for which was almost on them, would be followed by a period of torrential rain, and should reach the area of the *Amethyst*, the ship would have to be ready to manoeuvre, Kang or no Kang. In that event she might be able to slip away through the dense curtain of rain. The navigational risks, especially without radar, would of course be very serious, but the risk of being wrecked was a better prospect than that of surrender to Kang. In order to discover obliquely whether the Commander-in-Chief would approve, he sent him the following meaningful signal:

> Grateful your advice please on my actions if menaced by a typhoon. Have informed General on several occasions of this possible danger in order to hasten matters.

Two days later, after close study, Brind replied:

> Typhoons are unlikely to reach you in serious strength and you are in good holding ground. The golden rule of making an offing[11] and taking plenty of sea room applies particularly. We all listened to your special broadcast last Sunday. I hope you heard it all right and that another will not be necessary.

Not for a fortnight did Kerans perceive the hidden meaning of this calculated reply, and when he did he was full of self-reproach. The first sentence and the apparent banality of the last two sentences (which referred to a BBC 'Forces Favourites' programme for *Amethyst*), put in by Brind with a

---

[11] Getting away from land.

double meaning to fox the opponents, foxed Kerans also and, together with a signal made by Madden to Brind, observing that *Amethyst*'s anchor must now be deeply embedded and unlikely to drag, led him to think that it was his duty to remain at anchor if he could and continue to negotiate. He did not see that behind the veil, the true intent was in the second sentence. Lack of a code embarrassed all.

However, the possibility of escape as the only solution had been in his mind from quite early days. It would not have been in the traditions of the Royal Navy to have taken these gross indignities sitting down if any other course had been possible; but, since we were not at war, the prime consideration had always been to save lives, and the Foreign Office behind the scenes was reiterating its advice, 'Don't provoke'. However, Kerans now went ahead to reason the whole thing out, to calculate the factors of fuel, navigation, time, enemy reactions, 'deception' methods and so on. The time was not far distant, he could see when, *Amethyst*, having been reduced to the final extremity, the Communists would demand either acceptance of their terms or 'unconditional surrender'. The screw was already being turned harder. The ship's oil was again running very low. But, whatever he decided to do, he knew that he had the whole ship's company with him in the determination not to give in. He was confident that they would endure to the limit the abominable situation forced on them; but, as the perceptive Brind was able to discern far away in Japan, the strain of the heavy responsibility was beginning to tell on their young Captain.

The atmosphere had now become highly charged and a crisis was clearly ahead. When the summons came for the eleventh meeting at Chinkiang on July 23rd, Kerans accordingly took

Strain with him again.

It was to be the last meeting, and now indeed 'the air was full of swords'. At first Kerans took heart when he saw that Yuan was again in the chair, but, to his astonishment, Yuan himself went back on all that he had said before and took the complete Kang attitude. He would not accept Kerans's authorisation to negotiate except under Brind's personal signature; Donaldson's, which Brind had suggested, would not do. Nothing that Kerans said would convince him that such a thing was a physical impossibility. Moreover, he went back to the old cries of 'fundamental guilt', 'apologies' and 'compensation'. Confession of sin and submission to penance must precede any thought of safe conduct. Moreover, all four warships must now be put in the confessional. *Amethyst* was a hostage and would be held in bondage until the British paid the price of humiliation. It was the diplomacy of the brigand.

Yuan then expressed his displeasure at the British complaints against Kang, which he considered libellous, and, when Kerans challenged him on Kang's repudiation of the General's own formula of June 22nd, replied that Kang was his fully authorised negotiator and left the room.

There followed a two-hour slogging-match between Kerans and the Commissar, with which we need not concern ourselves. But at the end of it there occurred a revealing incident that showed even more of the man they had been dealing with. On this occasion, instead of the usual tea, Kerans and Strain were given a six-course luncheon, with Shanghai beer. While they were waiting for it, Kerans dozed off in a chair under the influence of the heat until suddenly the curtain of his drowsy senses was torn aside by the voice of Kang talking to Strain in perfect English!

'Are things really as bad on board as your Captain says?' he asked.

Kerans, having heard Kang say repeatedly through his interpreter for the last two months that he knew no English, sat astonished; until he recalled that the 'Major Kung' of earlier days had played the very same trick on Hett. But he made no sign and continued his pretence of sleeping.

Strain seized his opportunity. In bold, broad Scots, he gave the Commissar the full weight of the truth — half rations, food stocks getting lower and lower, no lights, no fans, the ship like the hot room of a Turkish bath, the men unable to sleep, cut off from their relatives, their last food in danger of going bad.

At this date, though he did not tell the Commissar so, their fuel was already down again to seventy-nine tons, and, when they got back to the wardroom and told the others that things were worse instead of better, Fearnley said:

'The only way we shall ever get out of this place is to make a run for it.'

CHAPTER 14: HOTTER AND HOTTER

THOUGH FUEL was badly down again and food stocks getting lower and lower, the spirit of *Amethyst* was not. If her ship's company had ever read them, they might well have echoed those memorable words of that great admiral, Robert Blake, when he lay in isolation and adversity off Cadiz in 1657: 'Notwithstanding the great tempests… we are all together and behold one another's face in comfort.'

They were in a more cheerful humour, however, than the scurvy-stricken Blake, living entirely on broths and jellies, and they made their little pert jokes on the trivial happenings of the day. The least occurrence that broke the tedium of the feverish heat became a topic of animated discussion. The goings and comings of Kerans and his chosen companion were watched with eager speculation. Kerans, with his secret thoughts taking vague shape in his mind, warned them to be careful of what they said, to be watchful also of the Chinese and the sampan women.

On July 13th their good spirits were freshly invigorated by a remarkable signal from the Commander-in-Chief which they all crowded round the notice-boards to read. With particular pride they saw that the signal was also distributed to 'All authorities ashore and afloat on the Far East Station'.

It was also very much intended, obliquely, to be made known to the Communists. This was it:

> For many reasons your situation is NOT receiving publicity at the moment, but I can assure you that you are very much in the mind of the Government and people at home. In fact the eyes of the world are on you. All your Fleet mates are

particularly concerned with your future and no effort is being spared to help you in any way that appears possible.

It is clear that the Communists have been holding you hostage to wring admissions from the British Government which would not only be untrue and dishonourable but would harm the cause of the Free Nations in the future.

No one can say how this will end, but of one thing I am quite sure, neither the British Government, the *Amethyst*'s ship's company nor myself will ever submit to threats, insults and perversions of the truth; nor shall we do anything to harm our country's honour.

You are always in our thoughts and I hope the accumulated good wishes of so many of us will cheer you up and give you confidence.

This signal from the Commander-in-Chief was very much a calculated step in the purpose that he had set himself of sustaining the ship's company and her captain in their firmness of purpose and their faith in themselves. His experience and his perception of events enabled him to sense the increasing strain and pressure upon men's endurance. 'It was quite clear to me,' he said afterwards, 'from reading between the lines of his signals, that Kerans was beginning to feel the strain, as any man would have done. That, of course, was exactly what Kang was aiming to do — to wear him down until, in a moment of desperation, he was willing to sign anything.' In their little, closed world, it was inevitable that *Amethyst*'s men should begin to feel how thin were the threads that held them to that larger world to which they belonged and which held all their loyalties and their loves. A tiny spark of doubt had begun to generate: were they becoming a forgotten ship? The long silence of the BBC over *Amethyst* was particularly felt. It was not easy to tell them that this silence was deliberate, that it was due to the anxiety of the Foreign Office not to endanger such tenuous negotiations as were being attempted by further antagonising the Communists. All this tedious wrangle over 'intrusion', 'invasion' and so on continued to be faithfully reported to the Foreign Office, and 'Do not provoke' continued to be the burthen of its advice.

To Brind's signal Kerans was therefore glad and proud to be able to send a perhaps even more remarkable reply. Having returned thanks, he gave a quotation from his quarterly Punishment Return (Form S.181):

> I cannot speak too highly of the conduct, bearing and fortitude of my remaining ship's company. They have endured a long period of hardships under almost intolerable conditions, and with cheerfulness and courage, which can have few equals in the time of peace. Many of them are new arrivals on the station and nearly all extremely young. British spirit in adversity has once again shown itself to be unassailable.
>
> This (punishment) return has been BLANK since the incident.

The next Sunday they had some light diversion. It was another blazing hot day. After Church, at which it was Strain's turn to read the lesson, all the ship's company gathered on the quarterdeck for photographs. Among plenty of merriment they were taken in groups —

> All the thin men led by the Captain
> All the fat men led by the doctor and the coxswain
> All the glamour led by Hett
> All those wearing beards
> All the Chinese
> All the others.

It was a pity that the Commissar was not there too. This July Sunday was one of their better days in this harsh month, for a consignment of emergency stores from Shanghai arrived, brought from Chinkiang by the faithful Leo. By an extraordinary twist of the Communist mind, they had been refused entry if consigned by the Shanghai Consulate (because they did not 'recognise' it), but when the secretary of the Shanghai Chamber of Commerce, Mr H. E. Aiers, was proposed there was no objection. The stores were mainly medical stores, disinfectants, toilet requisites, rat traps, a copy of the Chinese Commercial Code for use in signals; and from the Union Jack Club came sweets, cigarettes, papers and books. Every single box had been broken open by the Communists, but it was a good day all the same.

An even more unusual treat resulted from the luncheon to which Kang had regaled Kerans and Strain. On inquiry it was found that the Shanghai beer that was served that day was quite easily obtainable, though its price was 12s. 6d. a bottle. This, however, did not deter the ship's company and an order was therefore placed with the ship's seedy contractor. It was the first beer that anyone had had for ninety-nine days. 'I can't say,' said Frank, 'that it tasted any better than when we could buy it at 1s. 3d., but it was an occasion!'

Yet these demonstrations of cheerfulness were taking place during the very worst of the fierce, sultry heat, of which no better impression can be given than the simple entries in the coxswain's diary.

On the 18th Frank recorded:

Very, very hot. 90 days today and still going strong. I wonder how much longer that... is going to keep us?

And on the 19th:

What a night this has been, not a drop of wind anywhere, the messdecks are like an oven. Yesterday we set 52 rat traps, but with a nil result. I don't think you can beat the cat for catching them. Today is red hot again, and how it can get hot! This is by far the worst.

And on the 20th:

Midnight, and we cannot get to sleep for the heat... I am wringing wet through with perspiration, so I will go on the deck for a breather. Well, it is a damned sight worse now, even the vents are pushing hot air around. I am sure this is the hottest day yet.

On the 21st:

It keeps getting hotter and hotter each day, and they are finding it hard now down in the engine-room. Even on deck in the shade it is up to 102 degrees.

On the 22nd:

Things are beginning to get mighty uncomfortable and I'm afraid that if our oil gets much lower we shall be shutting down again for 48 hours at a time; then it won't be uncomfortable any more, it will be just plain Hell. Even to write this I have got four sheets of blotting paper under my wrist, and it is soaked through now... It is now beginning to get really grim.

They did shut down that night, and when Frank went to his bed he could hardly breathe. The rats still would not walk into the traps, but Simon had caught twelve.

Then there came a dramatic change. The sun lost its heat, the barometer dropped lower and lower, the sky turned to lead, a cold wind blew, and blew harder and harder. It was 'Gloria' on the way, and 'Gloria' was the code-name for the expected typhoon.

It had formed to the south of Formosa and its progress and probable future course were being carefully plotted by the meteorologists. It was moving north, with a distinct possibility that it would hit the China coast in the Wen Chow area. By July 23rd it appeared that it might pass over the Yangtse estuary. Madden advised Kerans that this would probably be during the night of July 24th-25th with winds of 80 knots and very heavy rain. So on the 24th *Amethyst* took precautions; the ship was battened down, all gear that might break away being screwed down, lashed or otherwise secured, the few remaining awnings furled, an anchor watch set and the engine-room ordered to be ready to provide steam for slow speed at short notice.

The night passed quietly, in fact, but on the morning of the 25th the weather deteriorated rapidly and it was clear that the typhoon was likely to pass fairly close to the ship. By 7.30 in the morning the wind was of gale force and blowing in very strong gusts of force eleven from the north-west, with the rain tearing down in dense sheets, beating on the steel ship with the sound of a kettledrum, and the waters of the Yangtse whipping up in an evil temper. The ship came to immediate notice for slow speed on one boiler and steam on the capstan. Special sea-duty men, for bridge, wheelhouse and tiller-flat, were warned to be ready, and at noon they were ordered to their stations. It was now getting exceedingly rough, the sky black as night, the shore only dimly visible through the curtains of rain, and the situation tense. The ship's engines were now at 'slow ahead' to keep the weight off the riding anchor. Just after noon the second anchor was let go underfoot to give further steadiness, but the port anchor, embedded now for over three months, was holding well. What would happen if the cable snapped was the anxiety that was in everyone's mind. They were threatened with destruction by the Communists if they attempted to move, but if the cable snapped they would have to move anyway. Only Kerans, who kept his thoughts dark, knew what he might do.

All day the storm raged, though it was only the edge of the typhoon that caught them. It was Strain's birthday, and also the day of his promotion to lieutenant-commander, and he celebrated it keeping two-hour watches on the bridge in a howling wind and drenching rain. On land there had been widespread damage. Roads were washed away and large falls of earth on the river's banks slid into the waters. Haystacks floated past the ship, one with an unhappy dog seated on top and another giving precarious passage to an anxious chicken. Pigs came swimming down, with one so close to the ship that someone tried to lasso it. Wreckage of all sorts was carried down from the stricken land and no living soul was visible except the sentry who kept faithful watch upon them.

At noon, during the height of the storm, Kerans received the following shrewd signal from the Commander-in-Chief:

I am very interested in how you fare. Typhoon Gloria has already been chasing some of us. I think you should be quite safe. My previous advice applies and you may think it wise to warn Kang that it may be essential for you to move downstream because of weather.

And he concluded:

I shall of course support your judgment.

Kerans read it through once and then again, slowly. It then dawned on him that Brind was trying to say: *If you see a chance of breaking out, go ahead!* His mind flashed back to Brind's previous signal about typhoon action: 'The golden rule of making an offing and taking plenty of sea-room...' He was very angry with himself.

By now, however, he felt that it was too late. The gale was still increasing in violence and turning the ship in the narrow part of the river would have been a lengthy operation. Visibility did not close down on the southern shore until two o'clock and then only for a short time. Not until then was the Communist sentry ashore, still at his post, obscured by the density of the rain. At that moment Kerans was within an ace of deciding to slip and make a bolt, and he signalled Brind:

> If cable parts will run for it. If wrecked and salvage impossible will blow up ship. Personnel to Shanghai.

The ship was, however, riding it out quite comfortably, and he had to decide that, if he were now to run for it, the ship and the lives within her stood very small chance of survival in her present condition. Turning in the river in gale winds with a ship so very light as she was would alone have been hazardous; but over and above that he was sure that the repairs to the shell holes near the waterline were nothing like strong enough to withstand heavy pounding from the seas at high speed, especially in the far rougher waters that must be expected when they reached the estuary. For he learnt from a weather report sent out by HMS *Hart* at sea that the centre of the typhoon was moving right across the estuary, somewhere just east of Kiang Yin. The ship, indeed, he might risk, but not the lives of the men.

So, while the wind shrieked and the rain lashed and the tumultuous river raced past him like a stampede of wild cattle, he rode out 'Gloria' with regret, feeling rather miserable, like a man who at the last moment decides not to jump a moving train. He *might* have got through with a great deal of luck. Should he blame himself? 'There is a tide in the affairs of men…' Well, he had missed this tide and there might not be another. He should have seen that the Admiral was prompting him. When, late in the day, 'Gloria' having gone, a signal in improvised code came from Brind saying expressly that his signals had been meant as sanction to break out, at his discretion, he was keenly mortified. Exhausted with fighting the storm and his own doubts, he went to bed. Next day he signalled his regrets and concluded:

I will not hesitate, Sir, another time.

Brind, however, concerned always to assess the strain on men's endurance and to sustain their fortitude, and anxious now about Kerans, reassured him. It was not an order; but he wanted Kerans to have the confidence of his support, if Kerans judged the moment right.

By Wednesday, the 27th, the wind had gone down and they were in for another hot, humid day, broken in the afternoon by the worst rain storm that they had had yet. The fight with 'Gloria' had cost them more than they could afford in fuel, which was now down to about sixty-three tons — the lowest figures yet recorded — and Kerans was again obliged to order heavy cuts. That day he received an exceptionally long and remarkable signal from the Commander-in-Chief embodying a dispatch for Yuan — the most categorical and forthright he had yet sent.

I do not recognise [he said] that the China People's Liberation Army has any right to detain HMS *Amethyst*.

It would be quite improper that the safe conduct of HMS *Amethyst* should be made conditional on admissions by me. It would be even more improper for you to make it conditional on admissions from me which I believe to be untrue.

I do not accept that our present discussions are an investigation into the rights and wrongs of the Yangtse incident of April 20th and 21st, 1949. This is for later discussion.

The subjects introduced by you are of international importance and far too high to be negotiated by Lieutenant-Commander Kerans.

Only within the framework of these principles, which 'accord closely with well-proved international practice and procedure', was he prepared to conduct negotiations.

To such lengths was Brind now prepared to go that he proposed to send in a special aircraft to bring the personally signed authorisation for Kerans, over which Yuan and Kang had made such a fuss, provided Yuan would give clearance for the aircraft.

More remarkable still, if Yuan could not reach agreement with Kerans on the basis he had outlined, the Commander-in-Chief was prepared personally to come up the Yangtse in a destroyer, if Yuan gave clearance for it.

Had he come personally — and this Brind obviously did not say to anyone — he was proposing, in default of agreement, to tell Yuan quite simply: 'I am going to sail *Amethyst* down-river tomorrow morning at eight o'clock and you will not fire on her.'

It is difficult to imagine how the Commander-in-Chief could go to further lengths, but Kerans felt quite sure by now that there was no likelihood at all that Yuan and Kang would agree to a British destroyer or aircraft being allowed in. That would be 'an invasion of Chinese sovereignty'. Kang did not want any big guns brought into the affair, on either side. *Amethyst* was his game, and he meant to have her. It was clear now to Kerans, too, that Yuan was a mere convenient figurehead in the business. It was the Political Commissar branch that was really concerned.

Kerans sent Leo ashore with the Commander-in-Chiefs memorandum the next day, but all his thoughts were now given to his secret design. For the benefit of the listening Kang, he built up a volume of dummy wireless traffic to various addressees complaining of individual hardships and shortage of fuel and stores, so that his enemy ashore should believe that his methods of psychological war were moving smoothly to their calculated end. At the same time Leo, on his behalf, made repeated efforts to hasten Kang in the matter of fuel replenishment, which was, indeed, a very genuine and desperate need; but he learnt that the Commissar had hurried off to Nanking on the 28th, obviously to consult the Super-Commissars. So much the better…

By now Kerans had begun to feel sufficiently confident about one factor of vital importance to his design — the establishment of a 'secure' telegraphic cipher. It happened that he was himself a trained cipher officer. The destruction of the official code books at Rose Island had been a severe embarrassment, for everything that was signalled could be read by the Communists, who must be assumed to be listening in. In the early days the only alternative to clear-language signals had been, on Madden's instructions, to employ certain technical manuals 'not likely to be possessed by a third party', but this was terribly cumbrous and not fully secure. The Government Telegraph Code, which was not a secret document and which had been retained on board, had, with certain modifications, been of help, but it was not sufficiently safe. Far away, however, the Commander-in-Chief's flag lieutenant, Lieutenant-Commander W. D. S. Scott, had been quietly working away, with Kerans's cooperation. at building up an ingenious system of ciphering, borrowed from the Germans, based partly on details of the next-of-kin of the ship's company and translated into groups of figures. On such slender threads hang these matters, however, that the system nearly broke down because one young rating could not remember his mother's Christian name! The system took a long time to build up by interchange of signals and was made more difficult by French's fatigue at this period. By late July, however, Scott and Kerans were understanding each other and the new private cipher was ready to be used.

Thus one problem was solved for the plan he had in mind.

On July 30th fuel was down to fifty-five tons. Subtracting sixteen tons for estimated loss by suction, this left thirty-nine tons. By nightfall, and after flashing up both boilers, there would be only some thirty-three tons, of which the passage to the open sea, where HMS *Concord* had now replaced *Hart* off the Saddles, would consume at least thirty.

This was the 101st day of the ship's captivity.

Before Kerans made his decision he reviewed all the factors that had to be assessed in determining it, if not in the manner of a staff college paper, none the less to good practical effect. It was early afternoon of a day of grilling heat, with the temperatures outdoor at something over 100 degrees in such shade as there was, and with officers and ratings disposed about the ship in the scantiest clothes and in various attitudes of surrender to the sun. The air was heavy with a drowsiness that did not encourage fateful decisions, and throughout the silent ship there was no life at all.

No one was more scantily clad than the captain himself. He wore only sandals, sun-glasses and a towel round his middle… He wanted to be quite alone for this secret session with himself. The heat could not dull or send to sleep the heavy sense of responsibility that lay on him; if he were to move now where his instincts were directing him, there would be at stake, not only his ship and eighty-one lives, but his country's good name also, for no one needed to be told that *Amethyst* was in the eyes of the world.

Kerans therefore made his way slowly forward past the recumbent bodies, the sun striking him like a sword. He reached the fo'c'sle and sat down on a bollard on the port side. He lit a cigarette and looked over the brazen scene, with the flood waters of the Yangtse rushing swiftly by. The monotony of the scene was only too familiar and he saw nothing but his own thoughts.

He now knew without equivocation that the Commander-in-Chief fully approved an attempt to break out at his discretion. The Commander-in-Chief himself was assuredly watching all the factors, knew what to expect, and when. Should he now exercise that discretion?

The fuel situation dominated everything. By some time tomorrow the fuel would be so low that there would not be enough for the passage to the open sea. After that, the ship would be immobile and dependent on Kang for fresh supplies. There was no promise or prospect of any more; still less that, if any were ever received, it would provide enough for the passage. Kang had no interest in giving them mobility.

Another compelling factor in the situation was the moon. A 'dark period' was very much to be desired, for a bright moon would very much endanger their passage across the front of the shore batteries. There had been a new moon on July 25th and this very night of July 30th was the most favourable there would be for nearly another four weeks. The young moon would set at one minute past 11 pm. After this night the moon would wax stronger and stronger and set progressively later, thus shortening the hours of darkness for escaping the enemy's eye in the long passage to the sea.

Even eleven o'clock, however, was too late to give time for the passage and get clear of serious trouble before daylight at the far end. For 'first light' next morning would be at 5.30 and the distance to be covered was 150 miles. With engines whose maximum attainable speed was eighteen knots this was an impossible task. By taking the risk of starting an hour earlier, he would have seven and a half hours for the race, and, although this itself meant a speed throughout of twenty knots, he knew that the swift following current would allow him to attain that speed, and even a little more, if all went well. All would have to go well.

Food was another compelling factor. Certain basic items, especially flour, were almost exhausted. The sugar and yeast had gone bad. Before the end of August there would be no more food of any kind and they would be at the mercy of Kang. If they stayed on another day, Kerans decided as he sat brooding, he would have to order quarter rations.

Such a harsh decision, Kerans felt, might place an unbearable strain on the men's morale, already severely tested by the exacting conditions on board. And there was the special and peculiar problem of Telegraphist French, who was beginning to wane under heat and exhaustion. He had already missed several passages on a certain routine and on some occasions recently the heat had so debilitated him that he could not write, the pencil slipping from his grasp.

These were the main arguments that led Kerans inescapably to the conclusion that they must go now — this very night — or go never. But, if the attempt were made, what were its chances of succeeding?

He shifted his position on the bollard and looked down at the river. The risks were formidable. A damaged ship, now riding very light in the water, manned by not much more than a skeleton crew on whom a severe physical and nervous test would be imposed, would have to run the gauntlet of the enemy guns for 150 miles in the dark over hazardous waters without lights or pilot, with imperfect navigational aids and inadequate charts and, for a critical stretch, no chart at all. That was a summing-up of the risks that faced Kerans as he balanced the accounts of his responsibility that fiery day.

Of the ship herself he felt reasonably confident. Her shell-holes had been plugged well enough for the present calm weather. To improve her stability in the water, he had been quietly removing as much top weight as possible during recent weeks and striking it below. The engines were in first-class order; although the brickwork in No 1 boiler had broken down, it would just about last for this one passage.

Given no severe casualties, the young ship's company would just about last, too. There would be enough hands to man only one 4-inch gun and one Oerlikon, and there could be no reliefs at all anywhere in the ship. The severest physical strain of all would be in the engine-room department, which would be seventeen hands short of their due complement, and they would be called upon for a tremendous and sustained effort in terrific heat.

As for the enemy guns, Kerans knew by now that, besides batteries in his immediate vicinity, there were others laid on for his benefit in the neighbourhood of Ta Chiang, together with a flotilla of small naval craft captured from the Kuomintang in the same area. Farther down the river, there would certainly still be batteries covering the boom at Kiang Yin and, most formidable of all, there were the permanent emplacements of 6-inch coast defence guns, with their searchlights, at the Woo Sung and Pao Shan forts at the mouth of the river. Kerans reflected, however, that, although the Communists had no doubt insured heavily for so valuable a prize as *Amethyst*, there would no longer be batteries all the way down the river, for the tide of war had moved far on. To a very large extent his chances of escape would depend on the degree to which he could achieve surprise and concealment, and his means of doing so had already been thought out; but that one hour before moon-set was going to be critical.

Whatever the enemy might do, however, he reflected, the navigational risks were undisguisable. For the fourteen-mile bend to Rose Island he would have no navigational help at all beyond the eyes on the bridge, watching as best they could for the dim, low outlines of the coasts on either hand, and the echo-sounder, warning him when he was getting into shallow water. Beyond Rose Island he had the Chinese Admiralty charts that he had kept so quiet about, but they were of low reliability. And he would have to take the whole thing at high speed. On the other hand, the Yangtse waters were now so swollen from the monsoon rains and the melting snows flooding down from the distant mountains that Kerans felt fairly confident that he could ride over all sandbanks, provided he could keep in the middle of the river. So heavy were the floods that the river level was now at least fifteen feet higher than it had been three months before and the ship was now a thousand yards from the south shore.

Neither chart nor any other navigational aid, however, would be of any avail to take the ship past what might prove the most dangerous of obstacles — the boom at Kiang Yin. There, to bar the wide river, a line of ships had been sunk some years before, with only a narrow channel through them to permit the passage of authorised ships. These sunken ships would by now have become deeply embedded and the flood-waters would have covered them even more deeply. But there was no knowing what new barrier the Communists might have strung across, and if there were no channel through, or if it were unlighted, only the most extraordinary fortune could save the ship. And this boom would almost certainly still be covered by guns.

These were the main points, many of them in his mind for a long time, that Kerans carefully reviewed in the solitude of his thoughts during that burning two hours after lunch on July 30th. By three o'clock he had made his decision. He suddenly felt very lonely and longed to confide in someone. All around him hands were lying about, drowsy and half stupefied by the sun. He called one of them and told him to ask Strain to come forward. When he arrived Kerans said to him very quietly:

'George, I am going to break out tonight.'

Strain, his submerged mind struggling to the surface of consciousness, looked back at him incredulously.

'Break out, sir?'

'Yes, it's like this…'

Before he had finished Strain was grinning broadly and his eyes glinting with excitement. Then they walked aft together and, in the new cipher, worked out between them the encryption of an 'emergency' signal to the Commander-in-

Chief and to HMS *Concord* off the Saddles. Kerans took it in to French and said: 'Make this as soon as you can. How are conditions?'

'A lot of atmospherics, sir.'

It took two hours to get the signal off, so that in the end it had to be sent by the top priority 'flash'. It said:

Top secret, C.-in-C., repeated Concord, from Kerans. I am going to try and break out at 10 pm tonight 30 July. Concord set watch 8290 [kilocycles].

CHAPTER 15: THE NIGHT RIDER

AFTER 'Intention' in military orders comes 'Method'. Kerans proposed, as we have seen, to move from his anchorage at 10 pm, an hour before moon-set, in order to reach HMS *Concord* (Commander N. R. H. Rodney) in the open sea beyond the dangerous Pao Shan and Woo Sung Forts by first light. There were three critical phases in the operation: first, the actual start and the twelve-mile, chartless passage as far as Rose Island past numerous batteries and the concentration of small craft somewhere opposite Ta Chiang; second, the passage of the boom at Kiang Yin; and last, the passage past the Woo Sung group of forts, with their 6-inch guns and searchlights — all very forbidding obstacles.

For the second and third risks there was virtually no 'planning' that he could possibly do. He could do no more than pray. For the actual breakaway, however, he planned very carefully. All the technique of stealth and silence of which a ship is capable must be employed. Not a sound must break the hot stillness of the night. Not a sign of movement that it was possible to disguise. Neither eyes nor ears of the enemy ashore must be brought to the alert. The very moment of starting would be critical, and the first thing not to do was to attempt to raise the anchor, for the rattling of the heavy chain-cable as it ground through the hawse-pipe would arouse every Communist within a mile. *Amethyst*'s anchor must therefore be left for ever in the mud of the Yangtse by 'slipping' the cable. To do this all that was necessary was to knock a pin or bolt out of one of the half-shackles that joined together the lengths of chain that made up the cable. The parted cable would thus drop into the water. Even this, however, involved a short length of cable passing out through the hawse-pipe, and to silence it Kerans, on some pretext, had caused the inboard length of cable to be bound round with bedding and greased. With all this done, there still remained the splash of the cable as it fell into the water. To prevent, or minimise, such a splash, the ship would steam slowly up to a point where it was judged that the cable would be hanging vertically, and at that moment the order to slip would be given.

So much for the most serious noise problem. Visual obscuration, however, was not completely possible. Even when the moon had set, good eyes accustomed to the dark would observe the movement of the ship against the water or the very low skyline. All that was possible was to deceive. Kerans had therefore decided to alter the silhouette of the ship to something resembling that of the landing craft which had been passing up and down and which he had been observing closely. To do so he would rig canvas screens from A gun to the extreme point of the bows. Thus he might pass as a Chinese ship and for that purpose he would be ready to show, if necessary, green-over-red yardarm lights as he had observed civilian shipping to be doing.

But, above all, he kept his thoughts utterly to himself as long as possible. Had he read the work of the ancient Chinese strategist, Sun Tzu, he would no doubt have recalled his memorable injunction: 'Keep your plans dark and impenetrable as night, and when you move fall like a thunderbolt.' That, indeed, is what he was to do. Hett was next taken into his confidence and the special task to which he was committed, in addition to his duties as Number One, was to memorise the whole 150 miles of the chart. Certain advance preparations would be necessary in the engine-room, quite apart from the raising of steam, and he therefore summoned Engine-Room Artificer Williams to his cabin at 6.30 pm and broke the news to him, ordering him to maintain complete security.

At 7.45 pm he ordered the coxswain to bring to his cabin seventeen Chief and Petty Officers and certain key ratings. They crowded into the little room, filling it completely, their questioning faces glistening with sweat and wondering what it could all be about. Were there to be new stringencies and privations? Was some further test to be made of their endurance and forbearance?

The answer came immediately in Kerans's first sentence.

'I have decided,' he said, 'to break out tonight at 22.00 hours.'

There is scarcely any need to say that every man was as though electrified. 'I don't think there was one of us,' said Frank, 'whose heart did not give an extra beat.'

To their intent and eager faces he went on to give details, telling them that the cable would have to be slipped, that they would have to risk an hour of moonlight and that they would have to pass Woo Sung by 5.30 next morning. From the engine-room he would want 'everything you have got', and if they came under fire he would call for black smoke. For additional stability, Nos 1 and 2 oil fuel tanks were to be flooded, in addition to Nos 7 and 8.

Normal wireless routine, he told French, would carry on until nine o'clock that evening, but after that there would be wireless silence until he gave orders. All signals would be by the 'flash' procedure, which took precedence over all other signals in the air.

Turning to Frank, he gave orders for the canvas silhouette screens to be rigged after dark, for all white paint to be blackened and for grease to be smeared over the shining brasswork of the sirens. No white clothing was to be worn by anyone on the upper deck. The utmost quiet was to be maintained and no use was to be made of the armament broadcast nor of the ship's inter-communication loudspeaker system. Some time after the ship had got under way, however, she might show a green light over red, and for these Chare would be responsible.

'If we should be spotted by the shore batteries,' he went on, 'and fired upon, guns are not to reply without my orders, because in the first place we do not wish unnecessarily to endanger Chinese lives, and in the second place the gun flashes would enable the shore batteries to lay more accurately.'

He paused a little and then continued: 'If the ship should be badly hit and liable to sink, our chief aim will be to save life. In that case I shall beach her, evacuate, set her on fire, open all sea-cocks, and then I personally shall blow her up. The ship's company, by whatever means may be available, either overland or in junks, will try to reach Shanghai. I think it is pretty certain' — and he learnt subsequently that it was so — 'that the RAF will be standing by with Sunderlands to fly in and take us off if at all possible.'

Another short pause, then: 'If I and Number One should both be killed, Petty Officer White will take executive command of the ship.' Dead silence.

'For that reason, Petty Officer, you are not to station yourself on the bridge.'

'I want you now,' he concluded, 'to pass this information on to the ship's company. I know we are terribly short-handed and it is going to be pretty tough for everyone, especially the engine-room department; but we have got to get out of this hole and I know you will all do your damnedest.

'But impress on everyone the need for the utmost security. Until it gets dark everything is to go on as it has for the last three months. I am specially nervous about the Chinese that we have on board. A chance remark by one of them to the sampan women, or even just an air of excitement, might give the show away. Besides, it is always possible that some of them may not be willing to risk their skins on this business and would give a hail to the shore. We can't chance that. So they must be carefully watched and if there is the slightest suspicion they must be locked up at once until we are under way.'

With that he dismissed them, simmering with suppressed excitement. While more than half aware of what the operation entailed, they were overjoyed at the thought of being up-and-doing, of 'getting out of this hole', and of proving their salt and their pride again. There was not a man of them who was not glad, or willing to take any risk to regain freedom. It was already nearly dark and every man went eagerly to his task, the sweat pouring from them, for even at that hour the outside temperature was 95 degrees. They had not much time for all that there was to do.

At the height of the preparations the look-out reported that the vegetable contractor, in a small junk, was approaching the ship in the dark. There was a moment's stunned silence. Then all preparations were immediately dropped, camp beds rushed on deck and the usual scenery and play put on for the ship's company to spend their night as usual. The horrible little man came on board but McCarthy met him at the top of the gangway with perfect self-control. When he saw that what the contractor had brought was a second consignment of the 12s. 6d. beer he smiled. 'Just the job', he thought. But, seeing that the man had not brought all the goods ordered, he most adroitly told him to come back with them *tomorrow*.

Then all went ahead again. The false silhouette was rigged; ammunition was brought up for B gun; Fearnley and Howell made ready their sick bay for casualties; the cooks, as for action stations, prepared a mountain of sandwiches; the echo-sounder was tested; the charts were made ready by Hett; Macnamara was brought up to the chart-house to be instructed; and down below the boilers roared.

At nine o'clock Kerans went on the bridge to accustom his eyes to the dark. He was wearing a borrowed khaki shirt and grey flannel trousers. Under acute tension, he was trembling inwardly. He prayed. Presently Hett quietly joined him, bringing with him in his mind a picture of the long passage ahead engraved with every detail. The look-outs followed. Then one by one each man of the depleted crew went to his action station, many to tasks that they had never done before. In the wheelhouse Frank stood at the wheel with two Boys at the port and starboard telegraphs. B gun and the Oerlikon stood ready manned. The fo'c'sle party gathered abaft the breakwater to slip the cable, connected to the bridge by a telephone specially rigged, so that orders could be passed quietly. French sat listening at his wireless set. Two ratings manned the echo-sounder, prepared to report its readings to the bridge by voice-pipe. Macnamara peered at the charts that he would have to follow. Below deck Strain, McCarthy and a small Damage Control Party stood ready equipped, at the word from the bridge, to move out to fight fires and damage anywhere in the ship. Every man worked quickly and in silence, his perceptions taut and responsive, obedient to every necessity. Lifebelts and steel-helmets were put on. In the engine-room four thousand horses stood expectantly in the shafts, waiting for the touch of the spur. The ship hummed quietly with the familiar pulse and undertones of her working life once more; she had woken from her long sleep and was ready for the race of her life. At every voice-pipe her ears stood pricked, waiting for the Captain's order to go.

Outside everything was very quiet, very hot, very still. The small, bright moon rode overhead, its light splintering in quick gleams and sparkles on the rushing waters of the river in high flood. The clock crept towards ten. Kerans, watching the naked moon, waited. A cloud was approaching. Wait a few minutes more.

But something else was approaching too. From ahead the silence of the night was broken by the distant mutter of an engine, and, turning apprehensively at the sound, Kerans and Hett saw a merchant ship rounding the bend of Ta Sha Island, fully lighted. They were to learn later that this ship of destiny was the *Kiang Ling Liberation*. Watching her intently, Kerans resolved his course of action. No danger this, but an opportunity. Here, for the most difficult part of his passage — for the fourteen miles to Rose Island for which he had no chart — was a heaven-sent pilot. He would follow astern of her. Picking up the telephone, he gave the order:

'Ring on main engines. Obey telegraphs. 180 revolutions.'

In the wheelhouse Frank acknowledged the order and passed it to the engine-room. The reins had tautened and the horse was ready for the spur.

Watching the merchantman, Kerans judged the time for his turn-round in the river. Then to the wheelhouse:

'Slow ahead, port. Midships.'

He heard Frank acknowledge and, as Williams down below in the engine-room opened the port manoeuvring valve, the ship began to glide ahead. Judging when the cable should be up-and-down, Kerans took up the telephone to the fo'c'sle party and gave the order:

'Slip.'

Not a sound, not the smallest splash, could be heard on the bridge as the cable dropped vertically into the water. Did it occur to Kerans, or to any of his shipmates, how symbolic was this act, this breaking of the chain that had held them tethered for so long in a vile pasture?

The moment the telephone told him that the shackles were off Kerans ordered:

'Wheel hard a-starboard. Starboard engine half astern. Port engine half ahead.'

Amethyst's bows swung off sharply 45 degrees to starboard and as they did so a fountain of sparks flew out of the funnel, sending every man's heart to his mouth. The damaged brickwork of No 1 boiler was the cause. But no one ashore seemed to see it. No shot came, no flare or challenging hail. The turn completed, Kerans ordered:

'Stop starboard. Half ahead both engines… Midships.'

In less than thirty seconds *Amethyst* was moving downriver, going slowly ahead on both engines, her bid for freedom begun. She was steaming at only ten knots, but slowly closing the merchant ship ahead. Throughout the ship every man was saying each in his own way: 'We're going — going at last. Thank God!'

For some half hour *Amethyst* pursued her silent, shadowy course. The gate of freedom was slowly swinging open. The slight wind of their movement blew refreshingly upon those on the upper deck. Nowhere was there any visible sign of life except the lights of the *Kiang Ling Liberation*. No sound broke the silence except the comforting hum of their own engines. The moon still shone palely in the sky. From time to time

Kerans passed a helm order to the wheelhouse, or the voice of the hand reading the echo-sounder floated up through the voice-pipe. All was going well.

By about 10.30 pm, when they were opposite Ta Chiang, where they knew there was a Communist battery, a flare shot into the sky ahead of the *Kiang Ling Liberation*, challenging her. She replied with the usual siren signals and altered course a little to starboard. *Amethyst*, now close astern of her, conformed with ten degrees of starboard wheel. At the same time Kerans noticed another small vessel on his port bow, fully lit, which appeared to be a landing craft — perhaps of the small flotilla that was known to have been assembled about here by the Communists as one of the agents of his destruction. A second flare went up from Ta Chiang, this time illuminating *Amethyst* and obviously intended for her. On the upper deck every man's face gleamed with startled brilliance and every detail of the ship's gear stood clearly defined. But she took no notice and went on her way.

Then the storm broke. First, the landing craft let go a burst of machine-gun fire across her bows. Kerans supposed that this was intended as a challenge to him to heave to, and he made ready to ram the craft if necessary; but, to his astonishment, he saw the fire to be directed, whether intentionally or not, upon the Ta Chiang battery. The shore batteries immediately flamed into life and in a few moments *Amethyst* came under heavy fire. From both banks field guns, semi-automatics and small-arms blazed and spat in a bewildering cross-fire. Kerans immediately ordered: 'Full ahead both engines.' Very shortly afterwards he called for black smoke and altered course fifteen degrees to port.

There followed a wild and confused fight, with shells and bullets flying erratically in all directions. At least four batteries were engaged, some of them directing their fire as much upon the other two ships as upon the *Amethyst*. The night was full of orange flashes and the swift flow of red tracer. Almost in the first minute of this melee *Amethyst* was hit, on the starboard waterline. The ship shook and heeled violently over to starboard. Kerans feared the engine-or the boiler-room had been hit and that the ship might sink. Not till then did he lean forward over the bridge and order B gun to open fire. On account of the heavy list, it could not do so, and only the Oerlikon and Brens were able to come into action.

Down the voice-pipe to French in the wireless office Kerans called: 'Make to Commander-in-Chief: *I am under heavy fire and been hit.*' The next instant he began a struggle to right the ship by weaving from port to starboard, but steering was desperately difficult, room to manoeuvre was small and in a minute the voice from the echo-sounder warned him that the ship had run into shallow water. Then, almost as suddenly as she had heeled over, the ship righted herself and B gun opened fire. By this time the *Kiang Ling Liberation* had switched off all her lights and had turned away towards the north bank. *Amethyst*, now working up to full speed and throwing up a great bow wave, raced past her with eighteen inches to spare amid a cloud of her own dense smoke. She passed on and ceased firing, B gun having fired only a single round.

But the little battle was by no means over. Looking astern, those in the frigate were amazed to see the shore batteries still heavily engaged. They were shooting at their own ships, and one of them, the unfortunate *Kiang Ling Liberation*, was beached and on fire. She was, indeed, to be beaten to death by the guns of her own side. The landing craft also seemed to have been hit, and it may well have been that the shore batteries thought that she was one of the ex-Nationalist ships trying to escape.

Looking round at the burning steamer, Hett said:

'Well, sir, there goes our pilot.'

'Afraid so,' replied Kerans, 'we're on our own now, Number One.'

'A jolly near thing, sir.'

Wellington had said the same with a different adjective. *Amethyst* had indeed made a miraculous escape. For once, fortune had been on her side. The plan to follow in the wake of the *Kiang Ling Liberation* had had its reward. *Amethyst* had profited from the confused situation, which she had confounded still more by her own devices of false silhouette and smokescreen. It is plain that the Communist gunners, used only to shooting at enemy infantry in land warfare, had no experience of this sort of situation, had no coordinated system of 'fire control' and had simply blazed off at everything they saw; to no purpose other than the destruction of one of their own ships, for which they were afterwards to cast the blame in vitriolic terms upon the British.

Away in Hong Kong the Commander-in-Chief had also been making his 'appreciation'. He, too, had been watching the moon, the fuel supply, morale and all other relevant factors. He, too, had seen what must be the deduction to which a balanced appreciation of all those factors must lead. Thus, even before the receipt of Kerans's signal, he was sure, to within a day or two, when *Amethyst* would attempt to break her chains; and he knew that tonight was the most likely of all. As soon as the news of Kerans's decision arrived, Brind informed the Admiralty and all others whose business it was to know this vital but secret news.

It so happened that for that evening Brind had arranged a small dinner party for about a dozen service and civilian guests on board HMS *Belfast*. He did not cancel it, anxious that, even so far away, there should be no possible cause for surmise. It was a very hot, humid night. The dinner ran its course and, precisely at ten o'clock, the moment that *Amethyst* was due to start her long night ride, the Admiral rose and said:

'Ladies and gentlemen, I should like you to think with me at this moment of His Majesty's ship *Amethyst*, and I give you the toast: "HMS *Amethyst* and all who sail in her".'

He did not, however, let his guests into the secret. The trials of the gallant frigate had for three months been an aching subject of discussion and it was not the first time that that toast had been drunk in Hong Kong. Very soon Kerans's signal, *I am under heavy fire and been hit*, was brought in to the Admiral, who excused himself to his guests while he read it. Then, at a hint from Scott, his Flag Lieutenant, the guests withdrew, the table was cleared, the charts laid out, together with rulers and dividers. Madden came in and the two admirals settled down with the Commander-in-Chief's Flag Captain, Staff Officer Operations and Flag Lieutenant, and with FO2's Fleet Navigating Officer and Flag Lieutenant. They were in white 'mess undress' rig. 'Thus,' in the words of the Commander-in-Chief, 'there was gathered round the table a group representative of those in the Fleet who had lived with the problems of *Amethyst* during the whole hundred days of her captivity, initiating negotiations for her release, doing their utmost in a diversity of ways to provide supplies, planning for the alleviation of the hardships of the ship's company, examining means of rescue and of help if she should run for it.'

Throughout the night the party sat up, receiving *Amethyst*'s signals the moment they arrived, following her course and her fortunes and anticipating events. Nor was this the only watching party that night, for London, Nanking, Singapore and

Shanghai, all of whom had shared the Fleet's anxieties throughout and had done their share in seeking to relieve them, were also kept informed of the stirring events of the night.

Brind's chief concerns were, as far as he could at that remove, to give heart and encouragement to Kerans, to provide for succour at the dangerous Whang Poo forts and to be ready for any other emergency action necessary. Thus, as soon as *Amethyst* had slipped, he brought *Concord* to immediate readiness, and ordered the Captain (Destroyers) of the Eighth Flotilla, in *Cossack*, at Sasebo, Japan, to close *Concord* with destroyers in company.

The hit that *Amethyst* had sustained proved to be less serious than Kerans had feared. It was a 'near miss' in the naval store that had opened her plates. Water poured in, but the hole was plugged and the pumps put to work. But it had been 'a damned near thing'. With the enemy now thoroughly alerted, Kerans decided that he must continue his passage at maximum speed, regardless of navigational risks and all the hazards involved. Besides, he had no time to waste if he was to pass Woo Sung before 5.30 am. Clearly, the Communists would now be waiting for their escaping prisoner with everything they had. Very soon she was racing through the night, 'making good' about twenty knots. Her engines were behaving magnificently under the care of their small, devoted band, working in a terrific temperature.

Thus *Amethyst*, her bow wave spreading out to break upon the shores like waves of the sea, raced past her old, unhappy anchorages, past Rose Island of evil memory at 10.50 pm, and far on again past Bate Point. No shot came from either place, their batteries no doubt gone. The moon had set, but from the bridge it was just possible to make out the dim lines of the distant banks of the river on either hand, and in the main reaches *Amethyst* knew she was reasonably safe in the centre of the Channel. Very soon she was 'making good' twenty-two knots, 'a bone in her teeth', steaming as never in her life before. Williams, wringing wet from head to foot, came anxiously up to the bridge and reported that water was flooding rapidly through the old wound in the tiller-flat. It was the most dangerous of all *Amethyst*'s wounds, but it was kept under control magnificently in a temperature of 120 degrees, with the watertight doors shut, by two very young hands who well knew that, if the worst occurred, they stood no chance.

Just before one in the morning *Amethyst* closed on her next danger point. This was the old Nationalist naval station of Kiang Yin, with the menacing uncertainty of its boom. As she approached, making smoke, *Amethyst* was challenged by flares from the shore, and when her identity was disclosed by their illumination immediately came under fire again, not only from the shore but from a ship also. A moment of dangerous uncertainty faced her. Unless the boom was closed altogether, she would expect to see two lighted buoys ahead, marking either side of the channel. She saw only one. Which side of this light should she go? On one side of it lay the safety of the channel, on the other Kerans knew not what. He asked Hett to confirm that he could see only one light ahead.

'Definitely only one, sir… Which side will you go?'

'Which side would you, Number One? It's anybody's guess. We'll leave it to starboard.'

He altered course a trifle and, arguing that the least risk was to pass as close as possible to the buoy, he gave the order to Frank through the wheelhouse voice-pipe:

'Port ten.'

'Ten of port wheel on, sir.'

'Ease to five.'

'Five of port wheel on, sir.'

'Midships.'

'Wheel amidships, sir.'

'Steer 062 degrees.'

Frank could not see what was wanted. He had but to obey orders. Completely calm amid the cannonade whistling just over the ship, he took her up at full speed, the buoy rocking in the bow wave on the starboard hand as she passed. Whatever boom there might be, *Amethyst* was through it.

Her speed and her confusing black smoke had baffled the shore gunners, too, and in a few minutes she was ahead of their line of fire, nothing visible of her except her dense train of smoke. She had been under fire this time for about fifteen minutes but had made no attempt to reply. Not a shell had touched her.

A little beyond the boom another danger appeared. Straight ahead was a small vessel, like a boom-defence ship, burning a small searchlight. She did not seem to know what was going on. There was no escaping her and surprise seemed the only course. Her heart in her mouth, *Amethyst* raced past her within a few feet, blanketing her fire and smothering her with smoke before she realised what had happened.

The river widened now and soon they could see neither bank, nothing but a wall of darkness ahead of them. But they drove on by the mental light of the memorised chart, a microcosm seemingly alone in the world. With the sweat drying on them under the speed of their onrush, hands on the upper deck suddenly realised they were very cold.

Half an hour later Kerans was able to signal to the Commander-in-Chief:

Half way.

And at 2.45 am, having completed 100 sea miles of his passage, he sent:

Hundred up.

Brind replied to him:

A magnificent century.

Magnificent it was, but the strain on the little ship's company was severe. The lookouts on the bridge, staring into the darkness over their appointed quarters, were drooping with fatigue, their vision blear and dizzy. In the boiler-room the temperature was 170 degrees, yet only two men fainted. Vomiting and prostrate, they were carried to the sick bay, where Fearnley placed them under fans and gave them salt and water to drink. They revived quickly, and in spite of Fearnley's concern insisted on returning to duty. There was no better example of devotion than the behaviour of these young men of the engine-room department. 'I felt,' said one of them, 'like a piece of melting butter.' Forbidden, of course, to drink plain water under these conditions, each man that night drank close on a gallon of tea.

In the enclosed wheelhouse, Frank still stood up at the wheel, after five hours of terrible strain and tension, wet through with perspiration and staring as in blinkers into the wall of darkness, seeing only straight ahead. 'I do not seem,' he recorded, 'to have a very clear recollection of what took place, lots of orders from the Captain and a hell of a lot of gunfire… but they would have had to blow us out of the water to stop us… more orders, more gunfire all the way down.'

He was to have plenty more orders. At four in the morning the bridge suddenly ordered 'Hard a-starboard,' and then immediately afterwards 'Hard a-port.' An unlighted junk had suddenly appeared out of the darkness straight ahead. Kerans, still steaming at full speed, did his best to avoid her, but it was too late and to his regret he cut right through her with a dreadful grinding of wood on steel that he never forgot. If there were any hands on board her, they could scarcely have survived.

The last hurdle — the Beechers Brook of this course — drew near. This was the forts of Pao Shan and Woo Sung, which Kerans regarded with deep misgiving. One direct hit anywhere from their 6-inch guns might cripple her. One on the waterline would certainly sink her. She would be obliged to pass Pao Shan at a range of less than two and half miles at about 5.30 am and he had small hope that their searchlights would miss him.

'I felt certain,' said Kerans, 'that I should come under fire here, and it was an uncomfortable feeling.'

He therefore decided to ask for *Concord*'s help and the following signals passed:

> *Amethyst* to Commander-in-Chief:
> Ask *Rodney* to cover me Woo Sung about 0530.
> Commander-in-Chief to *Concord*:
> If *Amethyst* passes Woo Sung near dawn support her by engaging batteries from seaward if they open pre.
> *Concord* to *Amethyst*:
> Can do.

At 3.50 am Kerans, not knowing exactly where *Concord* was, feeling now the long nervous strain, getting a little confused about exact timings and uncertain whether he would pass Woo Sung before first light, signalled to *Concord*: *Come quick*. Rodney, however, was already moving up to his support at speed.

At five o'clock every man on deck could see the searchlights ahead, sweeping slowly to and fro methodically across the area through which the ship would have to pass. It was an exceedingly uncomfortable moment. The cold, white fingers, searching ghostlike across the dark water, seemed inescapable and inexorable. Kerans ordered the engine-room to give him 'everything you've got — damage to engines accepted.' *Amethyst* raced on as she had never raced before, her engines at the utmost stretch of their power, her smoke a dark trail behind her. Everyone on board was taut and silent, B gun crew standing ready. As the ship came nearer, one of the long fingers slowly swung towards them and in a moment the ship was suffused with the cold, harsh light.

'It was,' said Kerans, 'one of our worst moments.' But it was only the 'spill' of the searchlight that caught them; they were not properly 'illuminated' by the direct beam striking them squarely. The main beam passed over them, leaving them invisible to the gunners ashore. It passed on and presently crept back. A second time, as they raced on, it did the same thing. 'The boldest held his breath for a time.' Not a gun spoke. Gradually the ship passed through the swept area, her tired coxswain still standing squarely up to her wheel, till at last the harsh glare was astern of her, her smoke now a safe barrier to its rays.

Ten minutes later the first faint gleam of day showed in the sky ahead of them and at twenty-nine minutes past five — within a minute of the calculated time — the distant outline of *Concord* could be seen darkly as the young sun suffused the horizon with a pale gold light. Kerans passed the news to the engine-room, and in a moment it had flashed through the ship and hands were calling jubilantly to each other: 'We're out, mate; we're out!'

Concord had seen her too, and Rodney, an old friend of Kerans's, signalled pertly: *Fancy meeting you again.*

To which Kerans, from the depths of a profound and inexpressible relief, made reply: *Never, never has a ship been more welcome.*

Amethyst was out in the open sea again, the wide and limitless sea, and she was free. She had broken the chain of her captivity and had left behind for ever the hateful river, the odious Kang, the lies, the spurious charges, the interminable wrangling, the squalor, the harshness of the life below decks and the vexatious inactivity. The salt water lapped her hull again and the sea breeze blew into her lungs.

Concord came up abreast and gave her cheer upon cheer, to which *Amethyst* responded with rejoicing and, we are told, some tears. 'I cannot explain,' said the hard-bitten Frank, 'how I felt when the Captain told me down the voice-pipe that we were out; I really don't know whether I wanted to let the tears roll out of my eyes, jump for joy, or just drop down on the deck with weariness.' We may well believe that their hearts were full. For not only had they regained their freedom, and come again among friends, but they had also the exultation of one who has run the greatest race of his life before the eyes of the world. Modest men that they were, they did not yet appreciate how high that achievement was to be rated, or foresee the tumult of applause that was to break upon their heads from all parts of the world from men and women who love freedom and admire splendid deeds. To all such men and women, watching from far away the half-told tale of the long harsh months of duress and the obstinate refusal to betray their country's honour, this superb and spectacular dash for freedom was the fitting climax and the just crown. As a feat of nerve and daring and seamanship, by a plain 'salt horse' and his devoted little ship's company, it has few equals of its kind.

So, in that July dawn in the freedom of the sea, with the early sun sprinkling the water with glints of light, the little company felt elation and a re-birth of life. Not until then, like runners who have run a race at utmost stretch, did the extremity of their exhaustion begin to overcome them. Hett, whose quiet fortitude and loyalty had always been so good an example, was on the point of collapse. Frank was grey and heavy-eyed beneath his jubilation. The hands who manned the echo-sounder had completely lost their voices. Kerans was drawn and strained. The sole spring of all responsibility, he had been under sustained nervous tension all night, never knowing what might lie hidden in the dark just ahead, and called upon, not only to plan and time for known hazards ahead, but also to act instinctively against any sudden hazard unknown. Upon none, however, had the sheer physical burden fallen more heavily than upon the engine- and boiler-room staffs, who, at half strength as they were and under young leadership, had endured a fiendish heat, dissolving in perspiration. Most of them were very soon to collapse. But indeed, all in all, the exploit had been a fine example of inspired teamwork by an improvised side.

Now, with the great race over, *Amethyst* prepared for her passage to Hong Kong to renew her life and duty. Her first need was oil, but as the heavy swell prevented *Concord* from coming alongside to replenish her, the two ships sailed quietly in company to the Saddle Islands. As they approached, Williams came up on the bridge and reported to Kerans:

'Sir, we are about to lose suction,' meaning that the last drop of usable oil was about to be expended.

'Never mind, *chum*,' answered Kerans, 'we are about to anchor!'

So, amid rejoicings, the scarred and rusty frigate and the trim destroyer lay alongside each other. All hands relaxed and Hett, before he collapsed and was carried to his bunk, took down Kerans's last signal to the Commander-in-Chief:

> Have rejoined the Fleet south of Woo Sung. No damage or casualties. God save the King.

To which, in less than half an hour, Brind replied:

> Welcome back to the Fleet. We are all extremely proud of your most gallant and skilful escape and that endurance and fortitude displayed by everyone has been rewarded by such success. Your bearing in adversity and your daring passage tonight will be epic in the history of the Navy.

PART THREE: EPILOGUE

CHAPTER 16: HOME IS THE SAILOR

'WHAT YOU have gone through in the Yangtse,' said Admiral Brind when he welcomed the ship's company at Hong Kong, 'is child's play to the publicity you are going to face.'

Never has a ship had a more overwhelming and spontaneous volley of applause than that which greeted *Amethyst*'s victory, for victory it was. Some 150 miles south of the Saddles, Madden joined her in his flagship *Jamaica*, and with his rare human touch gave pride of place ahead of him to *Amethyst* and signalled: *I am most proud that my flagship shares the honour of escorting your valiant ship to Hong Kong where the Commander-in-Chief is waiting to welcome you back to his Fleet.*

That was a knightly gesture characteristic of the man. No less warming, as they steamed into Hong Kong Harbour in pouring rain, was to see, hoisted by flags by the Commander-in-Chief, the rare signal: *Manoeuvre well executed* — 'the most pleasing signal of all that we received', said Kerans.

The rain did not damp the ardour of Hong Kong. Every conceivable type of harbour craft met the battered frigate outside the harbour and, with sirens sounding, accompanied her to her berth. Aircraft of the Royal Air Force flew overhead and dipped in salute. At the quayside to receive her were the Governor himself, the Commander-in-Chief, the General Officer Commanding, the Air Officer Commanding and all the dignitaries of the Colony. Many thousands of people, down to the humblest coolies, scorning the rain, poured from offices, warehouses and factories to line the eight miles of waterfront. The wet roofs of houses became alive with people. A fusillade of firecrackers began all over the Colony, the smoke from them so thick in places that traffic had to be stopped.

Far beyond the Colony, too, the news was crackling. 'The fame of her name' flashed into the headlines of the newspapers of every continent. A hail of telegrams arrived from all over the world, not only from official persons and from the sister Services, but also from the United States Navy and other foreign Services, business houses, the builders of the ship, municipalities and individuals of every station in life, whose imagination had been captured by the vivid exploit. At the head of all was one from His Majesty, who signalled to the Commander-in-Chief:

> Please convey to the commanding officer and ship's company of HMS *Amethyst* my hearty congratulations on their daring exploit to rejoin the Fleet. The courage, skill and determination shown by all on board have my highest commendation. Splice the mainbrace.
>
> GEORGE R.

Perhaps most touching of all was a telegram from the bereaved Mrs Skinner, who said: *Thankful for your magnificent escape. God bless you all.* The parents of Maurice Barnbrook, killed in the sick bay, sent an almost identical message. A party of Plymouth Wrens made: *Us be proud of ee.* A retired soldier unknown to anyone in the ship telegraphed: *I am only a pongo but I do congratulate and envy you.* And so it went on. Especially numerous were the telegrams that flowed in from Australia and New Zealand. Scouts, boys' clubs, schools joined in. The ship's notice boards were thickly covered. And when the mails began to come the volume was multiplied many times. Simon the cat and Peggy the dog alone had enormous 'fan mails'.

There followed, of course, junketings of all sorts, official and private. The Commander-in-Chief was right! Meanwhile, the dockyard engineers had taken *Amethyst* under their wing and were fitting her for the passage home to England, where she would have to go to be made fully fit for service again. Berger, her old pilot, recovered from his wounds, had rejoined from *Jamaica* at sea, and Madden's thoughtfulness had also caused all the rest of her missing crew, less those not yet fit, to be on board his flagship, and these all rejoined her in Hong Kong. Her old hands had been watching her fortunes with anxiety and with pride and rejoiced to return to their shipmates, some at least of them 'overwhelmed with emotion'.

All hands were sad, however, to say goodbye to George Strain, the 'passenger' who had embarked at Shanghai. He had been a tower of strength first to Weston and afterwards to Kerans, through the long captivity and through the great break-out. His leadership and his gift of imparting cheerful fortitude had been no less valuable than his ingenuity and his unwearied work upon the ship's equipment, including equipment that was quite outside his official scope. He became a watch-keeping officer and acted as such right till the arrival in Hong Kong. Under his eye and with the devotion and physical fortitude of Engine Room Artificer Williams and all hands of his department, the engine- and boiler-rooms, without whose 100 per cent efficiency *Amethyst* could never have made good her escape, were brought into harbour 'fit for a Commander-in-Chief's inspection'.

In late September, made ready for the long trip, *Amethyst* sailed for home. With some sad vacancies, her company were all together again, and, by happy agreement between the two Services, Fearnley sailed in her again. All the way home — at Singapore, Penang, Colombo, Aden, Fayid, Port Said, Malta and Gibraltar — the tale of welcome and applause was continued. Nor did it by any means end when at last she docked at Devonport on November 1st. Here there was a formidable welcome headed by the First Lord himself, the Lord Lieutenant of Devonshire and innumerable other persons of impressive importance. Then the ship's company marched through the streets to a civic luncheon. At Plymouth, Weston at last rejoined his old ship.

A little later, together with the ships' companies of HM ships *London*, *Consort* and *Black Swan* and the crew of the Sunderland, the City of London extended its cordial hand. Looking in superb shape, they marched to the Guildhall for a reception by the Lord Mayor, bringing a breezy air into the old City streets and a quickening of the pulse to their countrymen and women who thronged the route. Last scene of all was a march to Buckingham Palace itself for a special investiture and sherry for officers and their relatives with their Majesties personally. At this gathering the King presented Mrs Kerans with a watercolour miniature of her husband's ship, painted by an unknown admirer of the *Amethyst* in the Suez Canal whilst the ship was on passage home.

In due course, *Amethyst* herself renewed her active life and duty and returned to her old haunts in the Far East, taking part in the Korean campaign in 1951. In 1954 she went into Reserve and early in 1957, having for a brief while re-enacted the scenes of her ordeal and triumph for the benefit of a film, with her old captain acting as technical adviser and in command of the ship once more, she ended her honourable life — while this book was being printed — in the graveyard of the shipbreakers at Plymouth, within sight of the Mayflower Steps.

CHAPTER 17: WHAT THE COMMUNISTS SAID

THE COMMUNISTS, of course, were furious. The Yangtse was immediately closed to all traffic and for two days the Communist press sat in a stunned silence. The air was then rent with angry cries for retribution and blood, and for some time the British and other European communities, obliged to conceal their rejoicing, were in anything but a safe position.

On August 3rd the Communist New China News Agency published a report of General Yuan Chung-hsien's version of *Amethyst*'s 'infamous' escape. The quality of other Communist effusions on the subject may be judged when one says that this one is relatively mild and urbane in comparison with them. The errors in dates and names (*eg Companion* for *Consort*) have not been corrected.

PLA COMMANDER SPEAKS ON ATROCITIES PERPETRATED BY *AMETHYST*

NANKING, 2 August — Several hundred passengers on board the Chinese steamer *Kiangling* were drowned when it was sunk at 10 p.m. 30 July by the British naval vessel *Amethyst* which fled from a guarded part of the Yangtse River off Chinkiang, according to a statement made by General Yuan Chung-hsien, Commander of the People's Liberation Army at the Chinkiang front on 30 July. The *Amethyst* was crippled and captured by the People's Liberation Army when it invaded Chinese inland waterway and bombarded People's Liberation Army positions on 24 April.

General Yuan Chung-hsien stated that the *Amethyst* forced the passenger boat as *Kiangling* which was sailing down-river to sail alongside as a shield against shells of the People's Liberation Army and as a screen between it and the shore. When the People's Liberation Army discovered the escape and signalled for the *Amethyst* to stop, the *Amethyst* opened fire on the SS *Kiangling* which caught fire and sank.

While the People's Liberation Army men were rescuing the passengers of the SS *Kiangling*, the *Amethyst* swiftly sailed past the passengers in the river and fired on the junks engaged in rescue work. As a result, most of the passengers were drowned and only a few could be rescued while many junks were sunk. This was how the *Amethyst* escaped from the watch of the People's Liberation Army and fled out of the Yangtse River.

The British naval authorities conducted negotiations eleven times with the People's Liberation Army for the release of the *Amethyst* after it was captured, stated General Yuan Chung-hsien. The People's Liberation Army insisted that the British authorities must admit its error in the criminal action of 20 April and be prepared to talk on the question of reparations as the minimum conditions for upholding Chinese national sovereignty and honour before the People's Liberation Army would consider the release of the *Amethyst*.

The British representatives in the negotiations adopted the tactics of biding for time and evading responsibility. These negotiations have now turned out to be only a trick to wait for an opportunity to effect its escape.

Because of the irrefutable evidence, General Yuan Chung-hsien pointed out, Admiral Brind, Commander of the British Far East Fleet, cabled him on 27 July, three days before the flight of the *Amethyst*, and admitted that the *Amethyst* sailed into frontline areas without the permission of the Chinese

Liberation Army which had caused 'misunderstanding'. He made the same admission regarding the presence of the British naval vessels *London*, *Companion* and *Black Swan*.

It was evident, said General Yuan Chung-hsien, that the statement of Brind still did not admit the criminal action of the British naval vessel and slurred over it by calling it a 'misunderstanding'. The People's Liberation Army considered the statement by Brind unsatisfactory.

Three days later, General Yuan Chung-hsien pointed out, the British naval vessel concluded and exposed the insincere negotiations of the British Admiral by its infamous escape.

General Yuan Chung-hsien stated that though the officers and men of the *Amethyst* had shelled People's Liberation Army positions, the People's Liberation Army still treated them leniently. They were allowed to get their mails, oil and other articles of daily use from Nanking and Shanghai, and to buy fresh fruits and vegetables from nearby villages. People's Liberation Army men, who found two wounded British sailors along the shore, healed their wounds and sent them back to the *Amethyst*.

But now the people of China and the world have seen how the imperialists repay good with evil, General Yuan Chung-hsien added.

The officers and men of the *Amethyst* have made their infamous escape by shelling and sinking the SS *Kiangling* and many junks and killing hundreds of innocent Chinese citizens said General Yuan Chung-hsien.

He said: 'I firmly believe that the People's Liberation Army and people of the whole country will never forget to avenge those sacrificed. They will never forget and pardon the two savage atrocities of the British naval vessel, *Amethyst*, and its accomplices, the British naval vessels, *London*, *Companion* and *Black Swan*, and the deception of Admiral Brind.

'British Government, do not make haste in celebrating the success of the fleeing of the *Amethyst*. The whole case will not be closed so long as the culprits in the above-mentioned crimes are not punished and an apology and compensation for the crimes not made by the British Government.'

APPENDIX A: CASUALTIES AND AWARDS

KILLED IN ACTION OR DIED OF WOUNDS

Lieutenant-Commander B. M. Skinner, RN

Surgeon-Lieutenant J. M, Alderton, RN, MB

Sick Berth Attendant Thomas O. Baker

Boy First Class Maurice J. E. Barnbrook

Ordinary Seaman C. W. Battams

Stoker Mechanic Leslie Crann

Ordinary Seaman A. E. Driscoll

Ordinary Seaman D. J. Griffiths

Electrician's Mate First Class S. P. Hicks

Stoker Mechanic Victor D. Maskell (*assumed drowned or killed*)

Stoker Mechanic D. H. Morgan

Stoker Mechanic Patrick Muldoon

Ordinary Seaman P. J. Sinnott

Probationary Writer Edmund Tattersall

Ordinary Seaman D. G. Thomas

Able Seaman Albert A. J. Vincent

Ordinary Seaman George Winter

Ordinary Seaman Reginald J. Wright

Chief Petty Officer Stoker Mechanic Owen F. C. Aubrey

Stoker Mechanic William Barrow

Steward Leung Yuk and one other Chinese rating

WOUNDED

Lieutenant G. L. Weston, DSC, RN

Lieutenant (ND) P. E. C. Berger, RN

Lieutenant (E) E. G, Wilkinson, RN

Stoker Mechanic Thomas Anderson
Stoker Mechanic Samuel J. Bannister
Leading Seaman Arthur B. Crighton
Ordinary Seaman Amos W. J. Davies
Cook (S) Dennis Davis
Stoker Mechanic Ronald Fletcher
Stoker B. A. Loving
Boy First Class Samuel R. Marsh
Boy First Class Keith C. Martin
Stoker Mechanic F. W. Morrey
Acting Chief Petty Officer Rosslyn Nicholls
Ordinary Seaman Ronald C. Potter
Able Seaman R. G. Richards
Able Seaman Donald C. Redman
Ordinary Seaman Albert Rimmington
Boy First Class Brian Roberts
Ordinary Signalman D. W. Roberts
Chief Engine Room Artificer Stanley T. Roblin
Stores Assistant Anthony F. Silvey
Leading Seaman G. L. Stevens
Ordinary Seaman Maurice P. Tetler
Ordinary Signalman Douglas H. Wharton
Leading Seaman Cyril Williams
Ordinary Seaman Edward J. Williams
Ordinary Seaman Kenneth P. Williscroft

Together with a few slightly wounded, such as Stoker Mechanic George Maddocks and Stores Assistant Brynley Howell.

AWARDS

The Distinguished Service Order:
  Lieutenant-Commander J. S. Kerans, RN

Bar to the Distinguished Service Cross:
  Lieutenant G. L. Weston, DSC, RN
The Distinguished Service Cross:
  Lieutenant P. E. C. Berger, RN
  Flight Lieutenant M. E. Fearnley, RAF
Member of the Order of the British Empire:
  Lieutenant-Commander (L) G. B, Strain, RN
The Distinguished Service Medal:
  Acting Petty Officer L. Frank
  Telegraphist J. L. French
  Engine Room Artificer L. W. Williams
Mentioned in Dispatches:
  Lieutenant-Commander B. M. Skinner, RN (Posthumously)
  Surgeon-Lieutenant J. M. Alderton, RN, MB (Posthumously)
  Lieutenant K. S. Hett, RN
  Ordinary Seaman R. J. Wright (Posthumously)
  Electrical Artificer L. H. Chare
  Petty Officer W. H. Freeman
  Stores Petty Officer J. J. McCarthy
  Boy First Class K. C. Martin

In addition the Naval General Service Medal was awarded to all officers and ratings who had served in *Amethyst* at the time, together with those of HM ships *London*, *Consort* and *Black Swan*, and the crew of the Sunderland.

APPENDIX B: THE FEW

The following is the nominal roll of those who remained in the *Amethyst* after the evacuations at Rose Island and the Hsiao Ho:

Lieutenant-Commander J. S. Kerans
Lieutenant K. S. Hett
Lieutenant (L) G. B. Strain
Flight Lieutenant M. E. Fearnley, RAF
Leading Stoker Mechanic Denis C. Augustyns
Stoker Mechanic Samuel J. Bannister
Boy First Class David Bell
Electrician Hugh E. Blomley
Stoker Mechanic Arthur T. Brown
Ordinary Seaman James M. Bryson
Cook (S) George D. R. Cavill
Electrical Artificer Fourth Class Lionel H. Chare
Petty Officer Mechanic Leonard J. Connor
Ordinary Seaman Jack A. Day
Ordinary Seaman Kenneth Delve
Electrical Mechanic First Class Malachy Donnelly
Stoker Mechanic Albert E. Fellowes
Petty Officer Leslie Frank
Petty Officer William H. Freeman
Telegraphist Jack L. French
Able Seaman William Garfitt
Leading Seaman Mechanic Albert Garns
Boy First Class Bernard Grazier
Petty Officer Cook (S) George Griffiths
Ordinary Seaman Henry Harris

Leading Seaman George J. Hartness
Stoker Mechanic Charles A. Hawkins
Mechanic First Class Eric P. Holloway
Boy First Class Sidney S. Horton
Stores Assistant Brynley Howell (Acting Sick Berth Attendant)
Ordinary Seaman Rowland L. Hutchinson
Electrician Vernon E. Irwin
Ordinary Seaman Donald R. Jones
Ordinary Seaman John Jones
Ordinary Seaman Peter Jones
Ordinary Seaman Raymond Kay
Ordinary Seaman Charles A. Keicher
Petty Officer Stoker Mechanic George R. Logan
Stores Petty Officer John J. McCarthy
Ordinary Seaman Raymond C. McCullough
Leading Stoker Mechanic Duncan McDonald
Engine Room Artificer Second Class Ian McGlashen
Ordinary Seaman James McLean
Canteen Manager John J. S. Macnamara
Stoker Mechanic George Maddocks
Boy Keith Martin
Ordinary Seaman Robert M. Mitchell
Boy Ernest W. Munson
Chief Petty Officer Stoker Mechanic Jeremiah Murphy
Ordinary Seaman John Murphy
Ordinary Seaman James Nolan
Leading Stoker Mechanic T. Ormrod
Boy Colin E. J. Parish
Boy Wilfred D. Parnell
Wireman George Paul
Stoker Albert H. Pearce

Ordinary Seaman John Ray
Ordnance Artificer Fourth Class Trevor Rees
Boy Dennis Robert
Radio Electrical Mechanic Jack Rutter
Ordinary Seaman Eric N. Saunders
Boy Bernard Shaw
Shipwright William R. Smith
Petty Officer Stoker Mechanic William Venton
Able Seaman Jack Walker
Able Seaman Richard Wells
Petty Officer Alfred White
Ordinary Seaman Albert Williams
Engine Room Artificer Second Class Leonard W. Williams
Ordinary Seaman Denis Wilson
Ordinary Seaman Gordon Wright
Stoker Kenneth A. Winfield
Ordinary Seaman Thomas J. Townsend

APPENDIX C: INDEX OF CHINESE PERSONALITIES

(Approximate pronunciations shown in brackets)

Note. — 'i' as in 'eye', 'ur' as in 'earl' with the 'r' silent.

But Sai-tin (Boot Si-tin), Leading Steward — Captain's servant.

Chiang Kai-shek (Giang Ki-shek), Generalissimo — President of the Chinese Republic.

Chou En-Jai (Jo Un-li) — Premier, State Administrative Council (Communist) and Minister of Foreign Affairs.

Chu Teh (Joo Dur), General — C-in-C, CPLA.

Chu Wei (Joo Way), Lieutenant — First Grade Surgeon, 2nd Battalion, 177th Regiment, 59th Division of Nationalist 4th Army.

Jen Hsin-wrei (Ren Shin-way), Captain — Communist interpreter.

Kang Mai-chao (Gang Maow-chaow), Colonel — Political Commissar, 3rd Artillery Regiment, Frontier Headquarters, Chinkiang, CPLA.

Khoong Chung-tsung (Koong Jung-tzoong) — Head driver, ANA, Shanghai.

Kwei Yung-ching (Gway Yoong-jing), Admiral — C-in-C Nationalist Navy, Nanking.

Li Tsung-jen (Lee Tzoong-ren), General — President of Chinese Republic on resignation of Chiang Kai-shek.

Liu Chin-tseng ('Sam Leo') (Lew Gin-tseng) — Clerk in NA's office, Nanking, lent to *Amethyst* as interpreter.

Mao Tse-tung (Maow Dzur-doong) — Chairman, People's Republic of China.

'Mark' Meh (May), Captain — Chief of Staff, Nationalist Navy, Chinkiang Base.

Tai Kuo-liang (Ti Gwor-liang), Captain — Detachment Commander.

Wang Tso-hua (Hwong Tzaw-hwa), General — GOC Nationalist 4th Army.

Yuan Chung-hsien (Yuan Joong-shien), General — Area Commander, Chinkiang Front, CPLA.

A NOTE TO THE READER

If you have enjoyed this book enough to leave a review on **Amazon** and **Goodreads**, then we would be truly grateful.

The Estate of C. E. Lucas Phillips

Sapere Books is an exciting new publisher of brilliant fiction and popular history.

To find out more about our latest releases and our monthly bargain books visit our website:
saperebooks.com

Printed in Great Britain
by Amazon